Modern Scandinavian Furniture

Ulf Hård af Segerstad

MODERN SCANDINAVIAN FURNITURE

THE BEDMINSTER PRESS

© 1963 Ulf Hård af Segerstad
Design Erik Pettersson
Published by the Bedminster Press, Totowa, New Jersey, USA
English translation by Nancy and Edward Maze

Printed in Sweden by Nordisk Rotogravyr, Stockholm, 1963

Library of Congress catalogue card number: 63-11354

Facing the title page is an interior with furniture from the production of Nordiska Kompaniet. Background: "Triva" bookshelf designed by Elias Svedberg. The blue sofa "Villan" designed by Ingvar Andersson. The decorative enamel table top was designed by P. A. Törneman and made at Gustavsberg. The frame was designed by David Rosén. The armchair "Stor Eva" (Big Eve) was designed by Kerstin Hörlin-Holmquist, who also composed the furniture fabrics in the "Triva" series. On the shelves: a small wooden cross (called the St. Thomas cross) made by Swedish homecrafts. Flower vase made by Hertha Bengtsson for Rörstrand and blue vase on the table with enamel glaze by Carl-Harry Stålhane, Rörstrand. Oil painting by Torsten Dahl.

Contents

Peder Moos, Danish master carpenter, makes all his furniture by hand and devotes a great deal of thought to the design and finish. Each piece takes on the character of unique furniture sculpture. His younger countryman, Poul Kjærholm, designs furniture exclusively for industrial production, employing a metal frame. These two designers represent the two extremes in the richly differentiated Scandinavian furniture production.

Four Countries—
One Furniture Ideal

We spend a third of our lives sleeping. Naturally it is rather important to have a bed which provides real rest. It is a little more difficult to get accurate figures on just what portion of our lives we spend sitting in chairs or working at tables, but we do it often enough to be aware that furniture is not only one of the largest and most expensive items in our milieu but by far the most important.

However, these obvious practical considerations are not sufficient in themselves to explain the increased interest in furniture and interior decoration manifested by the general public during the last few decades. Of more importance in this connection, no doubt, is the fact that furniture helps us to create an environment which is pleasant, perhaps beautiful, or just plain individual. The affluence of our society means that an ever greater share of our population is able to avail themselves of this possibility. But at the same time, the old, reliable rules concerning the choice of furniture and interior decoration are losing their validity. A person has little guidance when furnishing a home. This has created obvious, and easily understandable, uncertainty.

Many people are wondering what has caused the present unsettled state of affairs in the creation of milieu. Architecture and interior decoration, during certain earlier periods, were marked by set rules and unity of style, because the attitude toward things which led to the creation of styles in turn became bound for varying lengths of time by the things themselves. A style change occurs when there is a revolt against the pressure of those things to which we have become attached but which nonetheless are anachronisms and alien. A new way of life calls for new forms and new things.

This is what is going on now. Economic, social and cultural changes are rapidly and radically reshaping the conditions and patterns of our lives. Things from a bygone generation do not fit. But a lagging production—from houses to ornaments—is still releasing antiquated goods on the market. The big push now in progress for new designs is necessary to overcome this and provide the market with things which truly belong to our time.

The design movement constitutes a part of the great transformations in society—economic, social and cultural. Different people have varying opinions about the significance of new design. Some are quite indifferent to its values and consider it of slight consequence in comparison with technical developments, for example. But for most people a feeling of well-being is dependent largely on the framework of their life, which is made up of the things around them. These things, comprising our entire external setting, are then an expression both of how an older generation lived and how we want to live today. At the point where these two intersect we come across the problems which each of us faces when we furnish our home.

Scandinavian furniture is currently held in high esteem in many parts of the world, chiefly because it fulfills many of the demands that a modern way of life has placed on furniture. An American expert has been struck by this very idea when he writes: "A piece of furniture from Scandinavia is practical, well constructed, unpretentious, thoroughly thought out and elegant. It can melt naturally into any sort of setting."

The Scandinavian "look" in furniture, then, is not a rigid style dictated by fashion. On the contrary, it manifests a desire to produce furniture without preconceived ideas or prejudice, furniture which satisfies the varying demands of our time. The best evidence of this is found in the fact that Scandinavian furniture actually has many different appearances. If this furniture has something in common, it is more likely to be found in its simple and straightforward anonymity rather than in a strikingly flashy design.

An individual piece of Scandinavian furniture, a chair, for example, can very easily be considered as an independent unit and be evaluated as such. But one's understanding of it is enhanced if one appraises it as an expression of a particular milieu, and observes it together with other furniture and furnishings in a Scandinavian home. Such a home in most cases will not be too different from a home in any other country with similar living conditions. But one could probably say that both the over-all effect and the details have been attended to with special care. The policy of design in Scandinavia aims at a practical and palpable way to "give each individual the possibility of a purposeful and happy life."

Scandinavian furniture production aims basically at putting quality furniture within the economic reach of every citizen. The color photo on page 9 shows furniture manufactured by cooperative concerns in Denmark, Finland and Sweden. The rocking chair was designed by a Dane, Hans J. Wegner, for FDB (Danish Cooperative Society). Sune Fromell, a Swede, is responsible for the design of the shelves, which are produced by the Swedish Cooperative Society, KF. The table and chairs in the background were designed by a Finn, Oiva Parviainen, for OTK.

The color photo shows a Danish
interior of a more exclusive type.
The desk in the foreground was
designed by Erik Riisager Hansen, the leather-covered easy chair,
"Ægget" (The Egg), by Arne Jacobsen for Fritz Hansens Eft.
A/S and the easy chair by the
window by Hans J. Wegner, for
A. P. Stolen. The shelves by Åge
Hermann Olsen.

The highly diversified activity which is characteristic of Scandinavian design in all its forms should, in reality, be regarded as a democratic-individualistic alternative to huge industries or government policies in some other countries, which force a more uniform product on mass societies. The Scandinavian view takes into account that people can have different ideas about furniture. Some people are clearly utility-conscious and think solely of the furniture's practical function and durability. Others want furniture with a modern, bold design, while a third group may put the emphasis on the cosy charm associated with furniture of a more traditional type. Furniture production in Scandinavia today is capable of satisfying all of these widely divergent tastes. It ranges all the way from time-honored handicraft furniture in wood to the extremely modern metal or plastic piece of mass-produced furniture. These varying forms of expression reflect the nuances inherent in a society dedicated to the freedom of the individual— where one wants to avoid conformity which infringes too harshly on one's personal way of life.

The aforementioned variations in the types of Nordic furniture are also nationally induced. Within the common framework each of the four Scandinavian countries—Denmark, Finland, Norway and Sweden—show independent features in their production. The history of modern furniture in each of the countries does not completely coincide. Sweden took the lead at the start of the current renaissance in the 20's and the early 30's. At that time, the byword was "Swedish grace" or "Swedish modern." During the last ten years Denmark has dominated the picture. "Danish design" is today synonymous with the highest possible quality. At the same time Finland is developing a furniture production, mostly industrially produced, which is replete with character. And during recent years Norway has made notable progress, especially with export furniture.

The best in Scandinavian furniture may vary somewhat in form, but even in the midst of this show of strength it retains the basic characteristics already mentioned. It is the result of a many-sided and reasonable attitude toward things which takes into account construction, choice of material, function and expressiveness. Such furniture does not pretend to be revolutionary. It has developed quietly and harmoniously, without extreme digressions. It is distinguished more by reliability than by spirituality, and the designer has not wracked his brains to offer novelty at any price. He has

The ideal Danish household has a distinctly middle-class air. The total effect is one of cultivated and unpretentious well-being. The various pieces of furniture are sturdily and carefully made. The style of furnishing, in which tradition is allied with moderate modernism, is worlds apart from superficial and fashionable affectations. The interior below is the work of Hans J. Wegner.

"Furniture should become more beautiful with use like well-worn sporting equipment," the Dane Börge Mogensen, has said. On this page is a section of the kitchen in his own house also serving as a living room. The interior shows traces of Scandinavian functionalism. The furniture, to be sure, is robust, but the handicraft quality has not deteriorated. Well-chosen materials and excellent workmanship are apparent down to the smallest detail in this room. The cupboard and drawers are dimensioned in accordance with meticulous function studies. Unpainted wooden ceiling, white walls and broad, fir floor boards have become characteristic elements in the modern one-story house.

Below: interior of experimental house for the Danish newspaper Berlingske Tidende. Interior decoration by Birgit and Christian Enevoldsen. Basket chairs by Palle Pedersen and Erik Andersen, for Klingenberg, Århus. End table by Börge Mogensen, for Fredericia Stolefabrik. Sofa by Illum Wikkelsö for Hjörring Möbel- & Madrasfabrik. Desk and shelves by Birgit and Christian Enevoldsen, for Havemanns Magasin.

It is important to point out that although Scandinavian furniture designs and interior decoration, to some extent, have regional roots, the outlook is clearly international. The interior created by Danish architect Arne Jacobsen bears witness to this, facing page. The chairs are a perfect example of his thoroughly thought-out and elegant standard pieces.

The steambath (sauna) interior by Lasse Ollinkari, left, is a modern design of a classic Finnish milieu.

In the Finnish furniture art of today one senses an affinity with the hardy primitivism of an earlier farm culture. The photo (right) was taken in the home of a famous artist. The rugged rocking chair and wooden slabs on trestles are a policy proclamation and a tribute to unaffected simplicity. The textile print on the wall is by Vuokko Eskolin and the ceramic figures by Birger Kaipiainen.

The Finnish architect Alvar Aalto also designs the furniture and other details for his buildings. In the early 30's he had already fashioned the prototype for the bent wood furniture which subsequently became characteristic of his style of interior decoration. This bent wood furniture coincided with the first big period of expansion in the Finnish wood industry and must be viewed in relation to its technical developments.

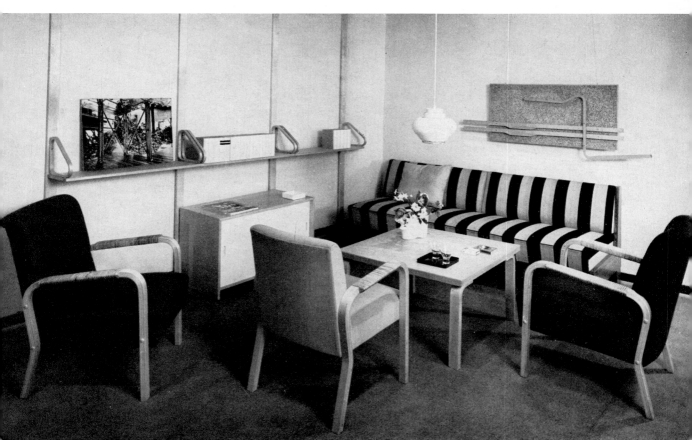

tried to carry out a job to the best of his ability, and that is all.

We mentioned earlier that the Scandinavian home is marked by a special solicitude. The reason for this is that the home plays a dominant role. The climate and the widely scattered and sparse population were originally contributing factors in the development of this tradition, which has been kept alive to this day. While people in southern countries spend the greater part of their time outside the home, circumstances are different in the North. Even if the Scandinavian climate with its snowy winters, warm summers and changeable in-between weather is far from unpleasant, it follows quite naturally that the dwelling there is regarded, not only as a place were one eats and sleeps, but as the true frame around family life. Further south one meets friends in restaurants and inns, but in the North one invites them to one's home.

Today Scandinavia is highly industrialized, but this development came late and occurred gradually, without the revolutionary effect which was characteristic of so many countries. So the old handicraft tradition survived. In any case, Scandinavians seem to have retained a bit of the warm "intimate feeling" toward the things around them. It should indeed be admitted that this attitude is not without its romantic or materialistic features. It was once described in the following way: "We still resemble our forefathers who huddled together in a safe little corner away from people, weather and winds. The fact that just such a nook is considered secure is perhaps the key to the Nordic world of form. The small scale, paying special attention to design details, endeavors with a modest treasury of form to create points of interest on which one's gaze can fall, within the limited circle of light cast by the evening lamp, and in this way to exclude the outside world."

Another important trait of Nordic furniture production is that it deleveped on a broad front. Everyone involved has worked for the realization of the goal: everyday excellence. Naturally some individual designers have acted as a driving force; but, on the whole, the furniture production is supported by the combined efforts of manufacturers and designers, researchers and technicians, theoreticians and consumer guides—and finally the interested consumer himself.

Interior of a Finnish house, Villa Pietinen. The easy chair in the foreground was designed by Carl-Gustav Hiort af Ornäs, for Puunveisto Oy, with leather cover from Friitala. The sofa and arm chair are by Kaarina Berg, for Haimi Oy. The table is from Askon Tehtaat. The sculpture in welded iron, "Hyena," by Eila Hiltunen.

With skill and consistency the Norwegian architect Alf Sture has
made use of the national characteristics of traditional Norwegian
interior decoration in creating the library shown above. The blue
painted chairs are of the so-called "jærbu" type; the untreated
wood is spruce. Counter to convention, Sture has used wood with
many and clearly visible knots, since this, not the so-called knot-
free wood, is authentic for this material. In the background: a
"Rya" rug woven by Anne-Lise Knutzen from a design by Knut
Rumohr. The lamp is from Sönnico A/S. The chairs are manufactured by Edv. Wilberg and the other furniture by Hiorth & Östlyngen.

The Norske Husflidsforening acts today as the principle steward of traditional Norwegian milieu. Interior decorator Aage Schou has been head of their design department for the last couple of decades. He has designed the oak furniture in the country estate shown above. The furniture fabrics and rug composed by Anne-Lise Aas.

The grand old man in the creation of Swedish milieu, Carl Malmsten, has executed this interior. He carries tradition forward, and his individual pieces of furniture, and interior decoration in general, combine Swedish peasant tradition with the culture of the manor house. For more than four decades he has fought for a more personalized home environment as a necessary counterbalance to the collectivization of communal life. Malmsten was considered a reactionary during the early years of functionalism; but now that the situation is more stabilized, his production constitutes one valuable element among many that go to make up the richly differentiated market afforded the Swedish customer.

22

The everyday Swedish milieu is
marked by simple, unaffected
comfort. The furniture is solid
without obviously extreme design.
The so-called "Cattelin" chair in
the photo, manufactured by Gemla, is a variation of the Tonet
furniture.

Opposite page: Thule's informal
conference room for important
visitors, with specially designed
furniture by Sture Andersson and
Pelle Åkerlund.

Wood–Past, Present and Future

This poem is written by a poet not a carpenter, but it bears witness to a respect and love for wood as a material which is shared by many designers and manufacturers. Scandinavian furniture production would not be what it is if this feeling for wood were not still alive. Another writer has contended a bit facetiously that furniture obviously ought to be made from wood, since nature steadily replenishes the supply, instead of from material which bereaves nature once and for all. The explanation for this firmly rooted attitude is to be found primarily in the fact that the Scandinavian countries are big wood producers and have behind them an immeasurably long tradition of wood. Modern industrialization has not violated this. On the contrary, it has incorporated many of the features which give quality to handicraft products.

Everything seems to indicate that wood, in the foreseeable future, will retain its place as the most important material in the production of furniture. However, the raw material will, to an ever greater extent, be treated and used in the form of veneer, plywood, laminated wood and fiberboard to mention only a few. If one examines a modern chair, for example, one may often find that it is composed entirely of wood products. The legs may be made of a solid piece of wood or of laminated pieces of wood. The back and seat may be of a molded fiber material and the padding of foam rubber, which is a wood product or a synthetic wood product. Both the fabric and varnish could be cellulose products. Furthermore, it is unnecessary to have a single screw in the chair, since it has probably been laminated or put together with tenon and mortise.

By nature, wood is a solid and homogeneous material, and in relation to its weight one of the strongest. When it is used as a supporting device, the sturdiness of wood compares favorably with metal because of its fibrous structure. Furthermore, wood has the important advantages that it can easily be worked with simple tools and that it is relatively light. In addition, it is a living material, with variations in color, grain, surface structure and softness which lend themselves to attractive finishes. It also ages well.

A decisive factor in the manufacture of furniture is that wood is a highly individual material. This means that one can choose the best possible kind of wood for each particular job. An excellent example of this is the so-called Windsor chair, which dates back to the 18th century. The sturdy seat into which the legs and spindles of the back are bored is usually made of elm or beech, types of wood that are easy to work with as long as the wood is fresh. But they become hard as stone when they have dried out. The curved arm rest is usually of long-grained ash, which is suitable for bending. The spindles of the back and arms can be of box-wood or beech, which are easy to lathe.

From an industrial point of view, however, this "individualism" of wood is a disadvantage. Solid wood warps, expands, dries and cracks. It is often said that it "works" or "lives." It is also difficult to procure wood of standardized quality in large quantities. Another difficulty is posed by the limited dimensions of wood. The supply of usable wood for furniture—knotless timber of large dimensions—is depleted annually. Nowadays the lumber is cut when the trees are younger, which means that the dimensions are steadily decreasing. In spite of modern, highly efficient forestry which is constantly speeding up the pace of exploitation, the price of timber has climbed; and today such indigenous Scandinavian wood as spruce, birch and fir are to a great extent just as expensive as foreign imported wood. The situation forces the furniture industry to work economically. This does not mean that the quality deteriorates, rather the contrary.

Laminated wood took a big step forward during World War II when wood began to be used even in the aircraft industry, where, for example, it proved itself to be superior in some respects to aluminum. Another wood product which has been utilized more frequently is fiberboard. This is produced from waste material which is reduced to pulp and then compressed. This product is for all practical purposes, "dead" and can be manufactured in almost any proportion or dimension desired. Moreover, the sheet can be easily bent into different shapes. In contrast to plywood, fiberboard lacks a natural wood surface and must therefore be painted or varnished to appear attractive.

A look at the history of furniture shows that different times and different countries have favored different kinds of wood, depending upon their availability, applicability for use in certain types of furniture, etc. Currently teak is considered to be a particularly characteristic material for Scandinavian furniture. Broadly speaking, this is quite correct in the production of the 50's. During the war years, manufacturers were restricted to the use of domestic material, such as oak, birch and fir. Quite naturally, when the war was over they turned with delight to the technically and esthetically satisfactory teak, which they could once more import. Things have returned to normal now, and manufacturers take a more balanced position. They choose from a wide selection of wood and gladly make use of domestic, light-colored wood. Even the consumer is beginning to overcome a former bias in favor of fancy wood, as opposed to common wood from temperate climates. Nowadays, one uses that type of wood which is most suitable for a certain job, and each type is prized for its own particular virtues. The result has been that furniture of domestic wood, such as fir and birch, is once again popular.

In our technocratic machine age with its smooth, shiny and sleek ideas of form, one can find traces of resistance by those who want to cultivate the value of the natural, untreated materials with their living structure. This conception is expressed in the current Scandinavian furniture production. Today's aim is to treat the wood in such a way that its natural features are brought out. Previously it often happened that the wood surface was painted or polished to make it harder and shinier, and therefore more resistant. Furniture treated in this fashion has, so to speak, two surfaces—the original porous, living surface of the wood, shimmering through the hard, glassy protective surface. This double surface is considered false,

Careful choice of materials and a technically perfect command of the wood's construction possibilities are apparent in standard-type furniture too. The teak chair on the left is designed by the Danes Nanna and Jörgen Ditzel, for Kolds Savværk. The leather-covered chair is a Karl Erik Ekselius design for J. O. Carlsson, Sweden. Moreover, both of these chairs possess the qualities which make them esthetically significant—good proportions and refined dimensions.

The color photo shows a selection of Scandinavian types of wood collected by Georg Bolin, the head of Carl Malmsten's workshop school, who is also known internationally as an instrument maker.

JUNIPER is a hard, slow growing type of wood with a characteristic spicy odor. Polishing gives it a smooth, silky-soft surface. Available in narrow widths only, it is used for smaller sloyd items.

ASH is easily worked, tough and supple. Used in nearly all areas of production, it is coarse-pored and well suited to current furniture ideals.

CURLY BIRCH is close-grained, hard and decorative. The irregular pattern is due to undeveloped branches, where the fibers have become intertwined. Sometimes it is used for making mallets and the like.

ELM looks much like ash but is not as tough. It can be used in many ways.

HORNBEAM is one of the heaviest, most close-grained and hardest types of wood. It is used mostly for tools, more rarely for furniture.

PEAR is close-grained and rather hard, with "short" fibers. Good for wood sculpture and for woodcut blocks.

BIRCH is one of the most versatile and most frequently employed kinds of wood in furniture making. It is easily worked, enhanced by polishing, and can be stained or painted. Especially suitable for slender dimensions and lithe lines, birch can take on a deep golden-yellow tone.

CHERRY is an exquisite material with a fine luster somewhat similar to elm.

APPLE is a close-grained, fairly hard sort of wood, similar to pear, but somewhat softer.

MAPLE is a heavy, hard and close-grained wood. It does not change significantly, retaining to a large extent its almost white appearance.

YEW is related to juniper, and its hard surface makes it suitable for such furniture details as handles, knobs, etc. It has usually been employed for tool handles.

FIR has been described as the finest coniferous wood in the world. It has a gleaming luster, and its living grain gives a decorative surface. Fir is strong, supple and easily worked. Often used in rather coarse dimensions but suitable for more slender designs as well, fir is stronger than mahogany and takes on a characteristic red-brown color.

SPRUCE is the most supple of all of the Nordic types of wood. Besides furniture, it is used for the backs of fine instruments, such as the violin. The annual rings are hard as steel, with soft material in between.

OAK is the most frequently used of the leaf-bearing types of wood. It is hard and rather coarse-pored but lends itself well to processing with various kinds of tools. Oak contains tannic acid and consequently is water resistant.

LINDEN is a porous, rather soft wood which is most commonly used for plywood and is also employed for sculpture.

RED BEECH is a heavy, strong, tough sort of wood. Since it does not absorb flavors, it is used in connection with the preparation of food. It is often used in furniture too. It lends itself well to staining and often appears disguised as mahogany, teak, or the like.

Arm rest shown at right is from chair on page 33.

in a sense, by our furniture designers today. Instead, the goal now is to utilize the new plastics, in order to develop a protective coat which is not detectable to the eye or hand and which preserves the wood without allowing any of its special characteristics to escape. The extremists leave the surface completely untreated. Certain robust, untreated table tops are meant to be worn, scratched and dirtied in order to achieve the natural beauty of wear and tear. They can be cleaned most simply by washing, or scouring and polishing, and are considered to become more beautiful with the years because of this rough treatment—like well-worn sporting equipment.

One important explanation for this, and for the fact that rustic types of wood like fir are coming into their own again, is that a second or vacation home is becoming more and more common. A good many people spend their free time in their own cottage in the archipelago, the mountains or the forest. Durable and solid furniture for these milieus is being produced on a mounting scale.

Even if one does not agree with the extremist attitude toward wood, it cannot be denied that wood is an excellent, living and "warm" material for furniture. This does not imply that wood is the only suitable material. Even in the 19th century, iron chairs were produced. And the metal tube furniture, which was introduced in the middle of the 20's and came to typify functionalism of the 30's, was the forerunner of much that is important in present-day furniture construction. Even in Scandinavia, metals and plastics are used nowadays for functional and versatile series furniture. This is especially true when it comes to furniture intended for the office, hospital and other public places. Scientific research has shown, however, that metal or plastic furniture, with few exceptions, is neither easier to produce nor more durable than wood. Therefore, each situation must be evaluated separately in order to choose the most suitable material. One thing seems to be pretty clear already: that metal or plastic can produce a rather cold and sterile interior, while wood, on the contrary, is warm and vital. This also helps to explain why wood dominates as the material for interior decoration in private homes.

The rather special position of the Scandinavian furniture market is also dependent on the structure of the production mechanism. In reality, the furniture is produced by a large number of very small workshops and factories. The famous Danish handicraft cabinetmakers employ an average of about 15 men. Paradoxically

Detail of an armchair designed by Carl Malmsten, Sweden, which illustrates how the form follows the grain of the wood and how the dimensions of the arm rests expand at the point where they join the chair back and the load on the arm rest is greatest.

The unique pieces of furniture by the Dane, Peder Moos, are a splendid illustration of wood at its technical best as furniture material. All his work bears the stamp of the highest handicraft ethics. The table and chair in the photos are, of course, one-of-a-kind. They could not be mass-produced, and the bizarre, luxurious designs stand out as extreme specimens of ultra-individualism. At the same time, the table design illustrates Peder Moos' tendency toward functional construction.

enough, the more industrialized outfits employ no fewer men. No less than 78 per cent of the Danish furniture factories engage fewer than 10 employees.

In Finland the situation is different. Here the market is dominated by a few larger manufacturers who employ 500 men or more. In Norway the market is divided up among a very large number of small producers. Among the 1,000 or so furniture factories in Sweden, only a couple can really be called large industries. The line separating handicraft cabinetmaking and industry is for this reason rather fluid. Generally speaking, both categories can boast first-class technical equipment. Under these conditions one will often find very little difference in quality between furniture which has been hand crafted and that which has been industrially produced. This situation has also had the happy consequence that men from industry and handicraftsmen understand each other to some extent and have bridged the gap encountered in other fields of activity.

From the point of view of efficiency, division into many small units is naturally a disadvantage. At the moment, attempts are being made to compensate for this by the merging of small companies into production groups; each company within a group will produce its own specialty. But there are advantages to the separate existence of so many small companies. In contrast to the big producer, for instance, they are not completely dependent on every product being a huge public success. They can experiment, vary their design, and successively adapt it to the changing market. It goes without saying that they try to avoid changes dictated purely by fashion. But of course it is impossible to eliminate these totally. If one takes a critical look at the current production, it cannot be denied that success on the foreign market has induced some manufacturers to speculate on a fashion—dictated Scandinavian "style". In principle, a design should be changed only when new demands on the furniture have made it obsolete.

35

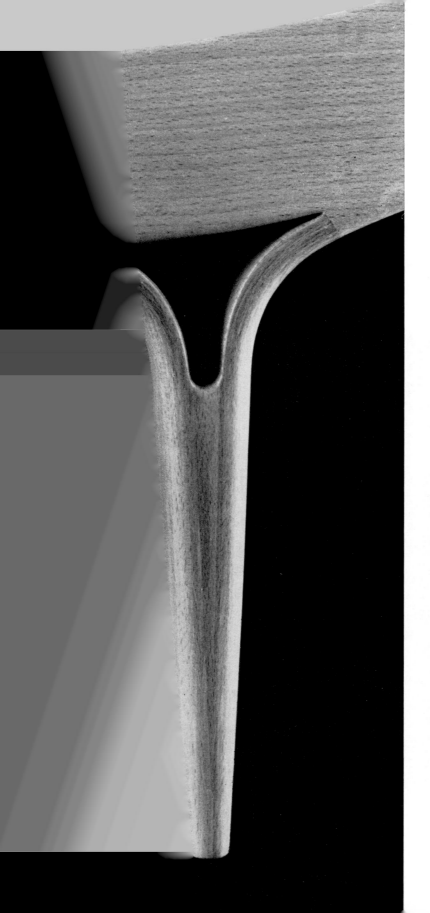

Quality, when it comes to material, technical construction and all-around design, is often more obvious if one examines the individual parts of a piece of furniture, rather than the piece of furniture as a whole. The leg—which Alvar Aalto calls the baby sister of the column—is used here as an object of comparison among three Scandinavian furniture designers who are totally different in their approach.

Around the middle of the 30's, Bruno Mathsson created furniture which was destined to become classic and which remains on the market in practically unaltered form after a quarter of a century. Pressure from the table top or bedstead is absorbed in the elastic fork of the split-top leg.

Josef Frank, who was one of the leading progressive architects in Vienna in the 20's, has introduced a measure of delicate Viennese elegance and polished internationalism to the Scandinavian furniture art. The slender dimensions and softly rounded design of the table legs on the right are typical of his way of handling details.

As an architect, Alvar Aalto constructs rationalistically but at the same time with bold intuition. The legs of his bent wood furniture, which fan out, with a softly organic movement to join the table top or chair seat, confirm this.

In recent years a number of young Swedish designers have worked with master carpenters, and produced wood furniture of an exclusive nature with advanced construction and form. The big picture below shows a cupboard in pear wood, designed by Hans Johansson and produced by Anders Berglund. It is joined without screws or glue and is held together merely by the tension between wooden ribs and framework. At no point do the material's dimensions exceed 0.8 cm. The details of construction and proportion enhance the piece and give it distinction. A detail from this cupboard is shown at the top of facing page.

The oiled birch sofa is designed by Stig Lönngren and made by Lars Larsson and master upholsterer Gösta Engström.
Bottom: mahogany stool, designed by Hans Kempe and Lars Ljunglöf and produced by David Sjölinder. The shape stresses the character of the material.

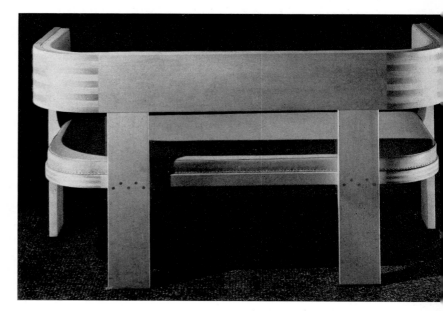

Three Ways
of Looking at Furniture

The first prerequisite for the purchase of good furniture is that
good, moderately priced furniture is to be found on the market.
Therefore it is in the best interests of all concerned that such production is encouraged. It has already been mentioned that the situation is relatively favorable in Scandinavia. There is probably no
other country in the world that offers the private individual a
chance to choose from such a superior assortment. The second
prerequisite governing the intelligent purchase of furniture is not
only a liking for furniture but also a knowledge of it as well.
One must be aware of the demands which will be placed on furniture as a whole and in particular; but one must also know oneself.
It is not the shape of the furniture or its arrangement in the home
which should determine a purchase but the individual or mutual
needs that must be satisfied by the furniture.

A Swedish art historian, Gregor Paulsson, gave some advice in
his book *Tingens bruk och prägel* (The Function and Design of
Things) about how one could develop this self knowledge. He
contends that we must judge all the things around us by three
criteria, each equally important. Applied to furniture this means
the following:

1. Furniture is meant to be used: the chair to sit on, the bed to
lie on, the table to hold china so that one can eat while comfortably
seated. These *practical* considerations mean that our relationship
to things and their usefulness is to some extent measurable in
absolutes. This seems obvious, but the world's markets abound
with furniture which is not made for practical use.

2. Furniture, like everything else around us, has a *social* function
too. It should be suitable for the place in society to which the owner
feels he belongs. One need simply recall how differently a chair is
designed in different societies and at different times. A royal
throne, for example, expresses the dignity of a head of state and
is consequently magnificent and expensive. In olden days these

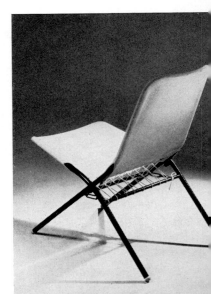

thrones often had legs shaped like animal paws, and the ends of the arm rests were likely to be decorated with lion heads, in order to make clear that the chair fulfilled a magic function and that the one sitting in it was protected by higher powers. Even today the chair of a leader bears some special designation that lends authority to the person seated in it. Much of the furniture passed down from previous generations was more an expression of the representative ideal than of comfort or practicality. We ourselves cannot imagine a chair intended for an elegant salon looking like a chair for a lodge, even if the demand for comfort in both cases is quite similar. The social quality is, in contrast to the practical, not measurable in absolutes. One cannot say that a certain chair is twice as suitable or unsuitable as another. However, one can say "I think" or "We in this group think" that a certain chair is more suitable or more appropriate than another.

3. A chair can also be used in a third way. When we let our fingers slide along a piece of finely worked wood, or feel the pleasant curve of an arm rest with our hand, or even just look at the pattern of an upholstery fabric, we are appreciating the chair *esthetically*. We think it is beautiful.

Anyone who is thinking about buying furniture can benefit by remembering these three points. They form the basis for a sensible approach to the question.

First of all, you should try to determine as objectively as possible the main practical requirements the furniture must satisfy. Is it really functional in the way your particular situation demands? Does the chair support your back properly? Is it the right height for your legs when you sit down? Is the table big enough to hold all of your paraphenalia? Can your room accommodate it? Is it sufficiently strong, steady and well made?

Secondly, do you have reason to ask yourself questions such as these: Does the furniture really go with my home environment? Is it in line with my position in life? Am I trying to "purchase" status which I cannot live up to in other ways? Is it in harmony with my other furniture and with the living conditions of my family and myself?

In third place come those questions which deal with taste and inclination. This does not mean that they are of less importance, only that they belong on the top of the question pile and not down in the foundations. In practice it is sometimes difficult to separate them. They are more or less interwoven, and affect each other.

These three folding chairs fulfill precisely the same practical function in similar ways. It would never occur to us, however, to use them in the same room. They belong to different social levels or regions in the home. The canvas-covered steel chair by the Swede Olof Pira belongs in the garden or on ship board. Chair number two by the Finn Ilmari Tapio-vaara is primarily intended for indoor use. It takes a minimum amount of space and is adaptable to many situations. The chair on top by the Dane Hans J. Wegner is almost prohibitively expensive and is at home in lavishly furnished libraries or other such places, where great store is set upon sound handicraft and exquisite detail finish.

Against the background of his divisions, Gregor Paulsson has also described different types of consumers. There is no space to include them here, but the author's conclusion is that our way of life should be self-determined and our goods selected accordingly. We should try to be independent, autonomous. We should not purchase furniture which makes us seem more elegant or more extraordinary than we are. Neither should we timidly let ourselves be bound to discordant conventions in our most intimate surroundings. Choosing goods implies choosing a way of life.

The question of autonomy is, of course, very complicated. Greatly simplified, the Scandinavian attitude can be summarized like this: In any debate about society in our day and age it is usually contended that the home should be reserved for an individually and personally constructed setting; this acts as a healthy counterbalance to the standardization and collectivization which is found where we work and in public places. Trying to stimulate the individual to furnish his home in a personal way suggests a sort of artistic acknowledgement of respect for the individual. At the same time, one should remember that the possibilities for this sort of individual shaping of the milieu are limited by different factors, not the least of which is the line taken by the manufacturers. But here again a balance must be achieved. It would be unrealistic to regard the home merely as a sort of "personality reserve." Advertising's persistent appeal to the individual often gives the consumer an exaggerated impression of his own importance.

At the time of functionalism's break-through thirty years ago, one of the fundamental tenets was that it was healthy and natural to be an absolutely ordinary person. The movement explicitly pointed out the importance of common utility objects. Designers and artists were encouraged to apply their efforts toward making these inexpensive items sensible yet beautiful. Simple materials and unadorned shapes were worshipped—at the expense of the more exclusive—because they expressed not only mass production as such but also the normal mode of existence. The modern goal was furniture for the "people"—primarily for those who previously had not had the opportunity to procure good, sensible furnishings for themselves because, at the time, such things were beyond their economic means. There was an idealistic purity in the program of functionalism, as well as in the designing of the things around us, which came as a result of this program, even if at times these things were artistically unsure or imperfect.

In the affluent society of today, there is a noticeable tendency to swing over to the other extreme. Nowadays that which is unique and exclusive is often sought out as something especially desirable. Consequently a considerable number of people are tempted to live beyond their esthetic means, so to speak. Here again, it is desirable to strike a balance between the individual and the mass. One chooses and furnishes according to an individual concept because it is natural; and it should express our collective living conditions. People living under similar circumstances have in all ages chosen similar forms of expression in their surroundings. It would seem desirable, when designing one's private milieu, to maintain one's own identity within the framework of the group. Here furniture plays an important role.

Perhaps in this connection the position of the designer in Scandinavia should be mentioned. Some designers work exclusively with mass production and mass distribution. The pressure of production forces its hard terms on their work, and they have little opportunity to exercise any radical influence on developments. Naturally it is good that mass production, with its advanced techniques, make use of designers who are aware that the standard of living is a form of culture which should enrich, not exploit, the life of the man in the street. On the other hand, there are artists who feel that improvements in the standard of living occur too slowly within the confines of mass production. They work for the precious few who need and have the means to procure the exclusively designed item which cannot well be produced on a mass scale. They feel, or at least hope, that the scope of their activities will be extended as the standard of living goes up. They can be compared with the art-handcraftsmen of former days. But in one respect they differ: their products are not meant to be part of the everyday equipment but rather adornments in the daily setting, which, in general, bears the traces of mass productions anonymity. There is yet another group of designers—still in the growing stages—who believe that these two points of view can be united right in the designer's workshop. Their attitude is humanistic. It springs from a conviction that a person should be able to determine his own surroundings according to his individual needs, without losing the fundamental advantages inherent in mass production. The future belongs to this latter group of designers, to whom designing is a comprehensive mission aimed at furthering social development.

Function, Design
and Quality

There is a joke about a Scandinavian furniture designer who once received an order for a bed from a young couple about to be married; however, the order was not completed and delivered until their silver wedding anniversary. The point of the story is not to illustrate how uncommonly slow the designer was, but rather how extremely exacting. To him the task of designing the home's most important piece of furniture was of such great moment that he must undertake careful preliminary studies and make exhaustive investigations concerning the bed's function, dimensions and suitability in relation to the home as a whole and the rest of the furniture in particular. Only then could he begin to think about starting the drawing job.

The episode could have occurred in the beginning of the 30's. Despite the exaggeration, this story has something important to say concerning the fundamental philosophy behind the new Scandinavian furniture production. Previously one "knew" rather precisely how a bed should look. The bedstead should be huge, ornamental and made of mahogany; and its size and adornment should indicate that it was the central piece of furniture in a respectable middle-class home. But for a number of reasons our designer could no longer see any sense in unquestioningly continuing to copy the old type of bed. In the first place, for some time, the new dwellings being built had such small rooms that an old-fashioned bed would have taken up an unwarranted amount of space. Secondly, the way of life for which the bed and other furniture was suited was slowly but surely changing. The obvious difficulty in getting domestic help, the working mother, and similar phenomena increased the demand for a house that was furnished more practically. Furthermore, one could no longer afford the old, expensive handicraft furniture. At the same time, technical developments had made it possible to produce simplified, standardized industrial furniture at a reasonable price. These events are well known and are part of

This detailed scale-drawing, by Danish furniture designer Kaare Klint, is one of the most important documents in the modern furniture art of Scandinavia. Kaare Klint carried out his first systematic function studies and measurements as early as 1916. As a professor at the Danish Academy of Art, his influence on the Scandinavian furniture art, both directly and indirectly, has been inestimable.

At the Dux factory, the largest producers of upholstered furniture in Sweden, a machine has been
devised to test the material and construction of
mattresses. The machine figure has the same
weight and measurements as "the average person."
Since the mattress is constructed to offer a physiologically correct sleeping position, one can, with
the help of the machine, determine how quickly
the material wears out and how much wear and
tear the mattress can take before it ceases to fulfill
the physiological requirements.

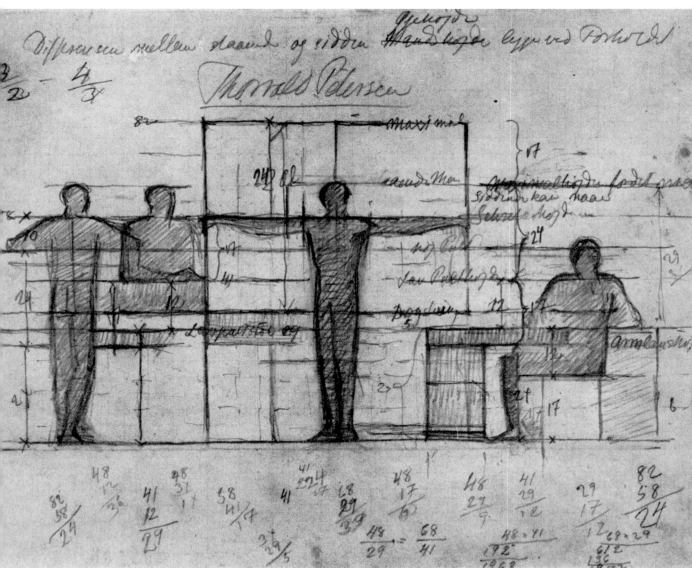

the past; but they are worth recalling, because the essential features in Scandinavian production still hold true. The significance can be summarized in the following way: furniture should not be created for a certain room but for a certain function. Every function should have its piece of furniture and each piece of furniture its function. Thus the earlier class distinctions in regard to furniture were done away with too. A piece of furniture was no longer "fine" just because it stood in a "fine" room, but because it fulfilled its function in the best possible way no matter where it happened to stand.

Of course, in this case a single bed was involved; but the designer naturally had the thought in the back of his mind that it could perhaps serve as a prototype for a mass-produced piece of furniture. For this series-type of manufacturing the design must be based on detailed studies, not only of the furniture and the use to which it is put, but also of the customer's or consumer's life, especially the housing conditions. In order for a chair, bed or sofa to be truly adaptable to a large number of people, the manufacturer must be aware of the variations in the human build. Furniture function studies have come to play an indispensible role among the complex economic, technical, social and esthetic factors affecting the manufacture of furniture. They have actually formed the foundations on which the entire new art of Scandinavian furniture rests.

Early functionalism in Scandinavia was naturally closely allied to functionalism on the continent, but even then there was a clear distinction between the two. A sort of symbol for functionalism on the continent was the Bauhaus school in Germany. The guiding principle here was that the designer must free himself from all previous thinking before embarking on a new assignment. He must eliminate all earlier furniture from his mind and base his solutions on his own original observation. The pioneers in Scandinavia were just as convinced that the new times demanded furniture of a new type. But instead of breaking completely with the past and disparaging its accomplishments, the Scandinavians chose the positive way and tried to learn from the traditional, building on it wherever possible. Consequently, Scandinavian functionalism was imprinted with the style's superficial trademark—geometrical design—only to an insignificant extent. However, the best Scandinavians were, in principle, no less radical than their colleagues elsewhere. They too sought the true synthesis, the self-evident answer to the problem.

Mogens Koch is an outstanding representative of the ingenuous, functional school of furniture-making in Denmark. Like his teacher, Kaare Klint, he is interested in ageless furniture types and furniture architecture of practical construction. This folding chair was designed by Koch in 1938, but was first put into production by Interna in 1960—an excellent example of fashion-free thinking. The upper part of the cross leg is bevelled to prevent the material from catching when the chair is folded. This unaffected, noble looking chair is architectonically, constructed throughout.

46

Under the auspices of The Swedish Society for Industrial Design, architects Erik Berglund and Sten Engdal have carried out scientific function studies concerning storage furniture, and have subsequently applied their findings in this series cupboard, "Contenta" for Johannesdal. Down to the smallest detail it is adapted to the storage needs of the normal family. Moreover, it can easily be built into the standard Swedish apartment.

The color photo illustrates the versatility of the "Contenta". The sofa was designed by Arne Norell and the armchair by Yngve Ekström. The "Rya" rug on the bed in the background is composed by Inger Sarin.

A chair became, if not an instrument on which to sit, at least a piece of equipment for sitting. A cupboard became a container built around certain contents. The best of the early functionalists had the ability not only to carry out consistent investigations concerning furniture function and practicality, but also to use the results as a framework on which to design beautiful furniture.

Following the breakthrough of the modern furniture art, a series of different tendencies came into play; but on the whole one can say that the designers focused their attention mainly on moveable furniture, especially chairs. Formerly these had been lined up along the walls and had, therefore, a neutral back side. Now they were pulled away from the wall and designed with all possible care, so that they would be interesting to look at from all sides. They have become an element in their own right in the room. Simultaneously the cupboard, which had been so dominant at one time, withdrew into the background and disappeared into the wall as a permanent fixture. The latest development brings the cupboard out into the open again, often as a room-divider between furniture groupings. Storage furniture then becomes more varied in the free, open, house plan so that it will not obstruct the view. The cupboard today is an important piece of furniture, perhaps one of the most important. In many ways it is a perfect illustration of the functional style of construction.

In the late 20's, Danish furniture designer Kaare Klint introduced a buffet which was half the size of the ordinary buffet model then on the market but which held just as much. The model created a sensation and has become a classic. The explanation for why Kaare Klint was so successful with his cupboard lies in the fact that he based the dimensions on extremely careful measurements of the household articles usually stored in such a sideboard. Klint's work has been carried on by his students in Denmark. Elsewhere in Scandinavia, especially in Sweden, similar methods have been put into practice quite independently. Let us take an example. How does one decide the measurements for a practical storage cupboard? First one determines what objects a normal family owns and needs storage space for. This will include the following items: clothes, linens, china and flatware; equipment for ironing, sewing, and caring for clothes; books and magazines; papers and documents; sheet music and phonograph records; spare bedding, hobby items and toys. In addition there will be groceries, kitchen equipment, cleaning apparatus, etc., which are usually classified separately. The

The pictures on this double-page spread show some of the many possible variations of the cupboard for linen and such: in the background there are bookcases and storage cupboards for writing materials, records, etc. Facing page is "Contenta", a dressing table in combination with a work table. Sewing corner is at right. The chair is by Hans J. Wegner.

51

sum of accumulated possessions decided upon after an inventory of many families then becomes the basis for measurements. Each item is measured and studied with an eye to convenient storage—in a moveable piece of furniture, in a built-in fixture, in a deep or shallow drawer, on a shelf or hanger, etc. Many variations in placement of all items in average supply are tested during storage-space trials.

A person's reach, eye level, standing or sitting work level, and space needed for cleaning have also been taken into account. Drawers, for instance, should be placed low enough so that the contents can be scanned easily. There ought to be open space in front of furniture, varied according to how high or low the piece of furniture is—partially to facilitate cleaning, partially so that drawers can be pulled out freely, doors can be opened, etc.

Furthermore, the measurements of storage furniture are dependent on ceiling height, length of walls, baseboards, doorways, and so forth. Different wall surfaces can be filled up with cupboards or shelves; and a natural harmony between the storage furniture and the other furniture must also be achieved. Scandinavian interior decorators have come to the conclusion that built-in furniture should be available for the bulkiest items and for equipment which most families will own in estimable quantities —for example, kitchen equipment, cleaning equipment, ironing things, as well as outdoor clothes and other wearing apparel. On the other hand, the family should be able to choose appropriate moveable furniture for those groups of articles that vary more in quantity or in some homes are totally non-existent, such as books, toys, and hobby items.

On the basis of their studies the researchers have concluded that the usual jumble of drawers, cupboards, bureaus and closets which cause goods to be more or less crumpled or damaged, are reprehensible. There have been various suggestions for replacing these with furniture that supposedly could contain all our worldly possessions in a more satisfactory manner. The relatively small furniture units, rearrangeable as a child's blocks, have many big advantages. Each part can be fashioned as an independent piece of furniture. But it can be combined with other parts, upward or sideways, and in this simple way enlarge the growing family's storage space. Frequently the fittings should be interchangeable, so that, for example, the piece of furniture could be arranged according to desire, with shelves, shallow or deep drawers, adjustable, perhaps

Danish architects Grethe Meyer and Börge Mogensen designed Boligens Byggeskabe (The "BB" Cabinet) on the basis of comprehensive investigations of the storage requirements of a Danish family. The cupboard's construction is clear and simple and as thoroughly worked out as the dimensions. Every detail bears witness to this. The doors are hinged on the side in such a way that they need be opened only ninety degrees in order to pull out the drawers. The keyhole is sunken to prevent clothes from catching on the key or damage to the wall or nearby furniture when the doors are open. This remarkable cupboard is constructed to meet storage needs in a small apartment, but at the same time is fulfills beautifully the important demand for handicraft quality and esthetic design.

by inches. A couple of small drawers could be interchanged with a large drawer. The width of the cupboard could be varied enough so that practically any wall area could be filled in completely. Even the height should have variation potentials.

With this solution to the storage problem the household is more sensibly furnished. The space is utilized more effectively, and the wasteful discard of objects when moving to another apartment is eliminated. The researchers leave the question of how storage furniture of these measurements is subsequently fashioned entirely up to the designer and manufacturer. They are free to make the furniture as artistic as they please. It is, in fact, impossible to produce furniture in a purposeful way without access to scientific, analytical results of this type.

In 1957, two of Kaare Klint's students, Grethe Meyer and Börge Mogensen, introduced the Boligens Byggeskabe ("BB" Cabinets), which is one of the best examples of how sensible furniture can help to promote the general standard of living. It is a built-in cupboard of a new sort; built-in in the sense that it can be constructed according to a room's dimensions, new to the extent that it can be disassembled again and moved, or even enlarged if desired. The cupboard is shown on page 53.

In Sweden, function studies have been carried out under the auspices of The Swedish Society for Industrial Design, with architects Erik Berglund and Sten Engdal at the helm. Their results have had a significant and widespread effect on furniture design. From the very beginning they made amazing discoveries. No one had suspected, for example, that the kitchen table—perhaps the simplest and most ordinary piece of household furniture, a slab with four legs—was available in over one hundred models on the Swedish market alone.

The function researchers asked themselves what criteria could be established for a proper table so that these might be used to judge the worth of those tables already on the market. They began by carrying out a vast number of measurements, proceeding from actual eating habits and table-setting methods. These resulted in a general picture of length, width, height, and extension possibilities generally required of any ordinary kitchen table. Hundred of people participated in the tests, and a recommendation was arrived at concerning the dimensions of such a table.

Strangely enough, not one of the more than one hundred available table models corresponded to the dimension require-

The small photo shows one of the chair testing machines constructed by Swedish architect Erik Berglund. How it works is described on page 57.

Both chairs on the facing page were designed by Gunnar Eklöf, on a special order from the Swedish Queen. The physiologically correct shape of the back is based on a thesis by Dr. Bengt Åkerblom, a Swedish physician.

Library table in solid oak, by Börge Mogensen, for P. Lauritsen & Söns Möbelfabrik. Mogensen designed a table as early as the 40's that stood out because of its daring massiveness. It was of Shaker type and is still manufactured, among others, by AB Karl Andersson & Söner in Sweden. Later Mogensen designed many tables, preferably in oak or other Nordic types of wood, and all were distinguished by an almost sculptural strength in the dimensions and details. Most of these tables—the one in the picture included—were first produced by master cabinetmaker Erh. Rasmussen, for the Copenhagen Cabinetmakers Guild Exhibit, and then manufactured industrially. The table lamp was designed by Kaare Klint and Aage Petersen, for Le Klint A/S. The bookcase in the background is part of the cupboard series "Öresund", designed by Börge Mogensen, for AB Karl Andersson & Söner, Sweden, as was the chair with seat and back made of cowhide.

ments. However, only one year after the research results were made public, 80 per cent of the total production met the new requirements and were approved, thanks to the position of authority held by The Swedish Society for Industrial Design and the excellent cooperation that had been established with industry. It should be emphasized that the results of these function studies are public information, available to all, and may be used without cost.

Earlier function studies in Sweden had dealt with bed measurements and types. They began by surveying the beds already offered on the market, and then took a look at sleeping habits, the room needed for bed clothes, the work space for making the bed, and the relationship between the size of the bed and the bedroom. This resulted in a recommendation: the normal bed should be at least $33^{1}/_{2}''$ wide, $35^{1}/_{2}''$ for a large person. The length of the bed naturally depends on the height of the person in question. One should add 8" to the height. An ordinary bed measures $33^{1}/_{2}'' \times 77''$. The bed should be $21^{1}/_{2}''$-$23^{1}/_{2}''$ high so that it is easy to make and also a reasonable sitting height. The bed should be 10" off the floor, so that it is easy to clean under it. This last figure is important. The current Japanese-inspired passion for exaggeratedly low furniture does not take these practical aspects into account. One forgets that the low Japanese furniture was created for a different manner of living than ours.

The latest function studies were published in 1960 in Sweden. These dealt with cupboards.

The Swedish researchers have also pioneered in the field of furniture durability. They have constructed a machine on which a chair, with a weight of 154 lb. on the seat, is placed. The chair is then tipped back and forth in the same way as it would be in daily use. The number of times it rocks is registered automatically. If the chair can take more than 25,000 rocking movements it is considered excellent. If it can take only 1,000—10,000 rocking movements it is recommended as a bedroom chair or such. Chairs which fail the test have one or more flaws in construction which can be localized by tests. The producer is informed about the chair's weak points, and in this way has an opportunity to correct them before the chair goes into production. Upholstered furniture is tested for durability in a similar way, with weights which belabor it as well as determine how much pressure the arm rests and framework can take. Norms are now being worked out for the height and inclination of the seat, the height and shape of the back, the length and shape of the arm rests, durability of the upholstery, solidity of the arm rests, etc. Similiar mechanical methods have been used to test the resistance-capacity of table surfaces to liquids, blows, jolts, etc.

General space requirements have been coordinated with the findings of housing researchers. Private experts have investigated the height of a chair, the shape of the back rest, etc., from a medical point of view. The first such tests were made by a Danish doctor, Egil Snorrasson, and a Swedish doctor, Bengt Åkerblom.

What the consumer expects from a piece of furniture can be summarized in the question: What returns will I get from this piece of furniture for the price I must pay?

The usefulness of the product must form the basis for an opinion. Measurements are vital in this connection: a big enough table top, the correct chair height, a sufficiently roomy cupboard, the comfortably wide bed. Normally the correct measurements are no more expensive than the incorrect measurements. Therefore, we have a right to expect them, even in inexpensive furniture. The Swedish studies have shown that many manufacturers of tables, however, use unsuitable measurements, simply because they can get four table tops instead of three from raw material of a certain size. Big savings for the consumer could be made if there were fewer variations in measurements, if the measurements of the furniture and the raw material were coordinated, if different manufacturers coordinated the measurements of their products, etc.

The next thing a consumer looks for in a product is durability. Here the purchaser has reason to be on his guard. Tests have shown objectively that durability is not guaranteed by higher price. The reasons why a chair falls apart are many, and few of them have anything to do with price. Most commonly the difficulty has to do with faulty joining because of some mechanical failure. Some chairs fall apart because the glue is incorrect. Working with the glue manufacturers can prove valuable in this connection. The dimensions of a chair may be too frail. The cost of reinforcing the weak sections is usually insignificant and will scarcely effect the final price.

The price of the wood itself is not a decisive factor. The more expensive kinds of wood tend to be the least durable. Beech, birch, and oak are, in general, the strongest and the cheapest. Similarly, the more expensive methods of finishing are the least durable.

But there certainly must be some sort of difference between the more expensive and least expensive furniture? The quality we can expect in more expensive furniture is a more attractive appearance —better design, more beautiful material, pleasing touch. All of this can cost money. Compare two chests. The one is made of carefully selected material—veneer with an even, uniform structure, put together without visible seams and with a smooth surface unmarked by the material beneath; the edging of the same color as the veneer; the edges rounded off evenly and consistently; finished underneath in accessible spots; the fittings meticulously chosen and everything nicely joined together with screws of the right size that are put in correctly; drawers that slide easily and smoothly and are finished on the inside. Quality cabinet-making like this is largely a matter of esthetics; and, within reason, we can expect to pay for it.

What the consumer has a right to complain about is quality which is lower than it should be in any price range—carelessness, cheating, lack of attention to measurements and details, inexcusable ignorance; and, especially, neglecting to inform the purchaser about the true qualities of the product. Generally speaking, a layman cannot judge the durability of a piece of furniture just by studying and checking the workmanship. A chair that to all appearances seems first-class may be marred by concealed defects, like unsuitable glue, or imperceptible weaknesses in the material which can only be detected by systematic mechanical tests. Thus the consumer should demand a product declaration; but, as yet, even in Sweden, only a small share of the furniture on the market has undergone testing. Such a product declaration must always be based on factual information—in this case measurable machine tests. However, until such a time as these declarations are available, the customer must be satisfied with information which can be gleaned from a furniture dealer who has a sense of responsibility. It seems obvious that in a civilized community the consumer should be able to expect reliable service and advice from the agency acting as middleman between the producer and the consumer. Finally the producer, perhaps with the designer as a go-between, must accept full responsibility toward the consumer. With these goals, one can hope that eventually "luxury" will be accessible to all—that is, if one uses the world "luxury" to mean, not pomp, but the best quality at a given price.

Furniture Buying Guide

DINING TABLES

Is the table big enough?

Figure on 23″ per person around the perimeter of the table. The width of the table must be no less than 29$^{1}/_{2}$″, so that two places can be set opposite one another. If space is limited, choose a chair with a seat which is shallower from front to back, rather than a narrower table. Only if the table is at least 33$^{1}/_{2}$″ wide can one make use of the space between the place settings for flowers, candles, etc. A square table for 4 people should be 40″ × 40″. If it is equipped with drop leaves, there will be room for 8 people. A round table that measures 43$^{1}/_{2}$″ in diameter can seat 4–5 persons. Provided with two extra leaves, each 14″, there will be room for 10 persons. A round table with a diameter of 47$^{1}/_{2}$″ seats 6 persons. With a 40″ leaf it seats 10.

Are you seated comfortably?

The table legs must not be in the way even when the leaves are added to the table. There should be at least 26″ of leg room under the table.

Is the height right?

The normal height is about 28$^{1}/_{2}$″. The table should be 10$^{1}/_{2}$″-11$^{1}/_{2}$″ higher than the chair seats.

Is the table solid?

Grasp the table top and shake it; then you can feel whether it is solid or weak.

How durable is the finish on the table top?

There are three main types of finishes that are used in the furniture industry today: cellulose lacquer, plastic lacquer, and, to a lesser extent, oil. Cellulose lacquer is inexpensive, fairly durable and, with the proper treatment, can give a beautiful surface on which small blemishes can be touched up. It has a tendency to yellow and after a time become brittle. The latest plastic lacquers give a strong, durable surface that can really take rough treatment, even a burning cigarette. A soft, non-drying film distinguishes an oil finish from the others. It is a sort of impregnation and must

60

be touched up every so often. An oiled wood surface cannot resist damage from heat and liquids, but it is easy to touch up. On the whole, thin finishes are often easily damaged by liquids, and thick finishes scratch easily.

Is the table top level?   Let the light from a window reflect on the table top. This brings out any unevenness or other flaws. Run the palm of the hand over the surface. You should not feel any blisters, cracks or seams where the pieces of veneer join. A table with a veneer surface is sensitive to blows. The underlying wood or veneer core, composed of either plywood or fiberboard, cannot be seen at all on this sort of table top, because the edges must be protected by glued strips of veneer edging. This acts as a protection against bumps, blows, and splitting of the veneer.

If a table top is of solid wood, the line of the annual rings and the joints of the solid block will be seen on the short vertical edge of the table top. A solid slab which has been joined in a technically correct manner has even, uniform markings, with the annual rings running mostly parallel to one another. A slab which has been incorrectly joined has a turbulent, uneven appearance. To obtain a fine solid wood table top it is imperative that the selection of wood and the joining are first-class. A table top with a good veneer is often more smooth and level, and it holds its shape better. A table with a solid wood top should not stand too near radiators. A well-made table is finished to some extent even on the underside. One should be able to run the hand over the table's underside without getting splinters in the fingers.

Other design considerations   Remember that a round table takes up more room than a square one.

OTHER TABLES

Is the height right?   A good height for a desk is $28^{1}/_{2}''$, for a typewriter table $25^{1}/_{2}''$, sewing machine table $27^{1}/_{2}''$, end table $21^{1}/_{2}''$-$23''$, bedstand $4''$ higher than the bed.

Is the table steady?   A work table is more stable if it rests on a cabinet or set of drawers.

Small tables for the radio or TV ought to be very steady. Vibrations are particularly disturbing in the case of TV. In addition to what has already been said concerning durability, one must count on needing a really serviceable surface on a work table. A laminated plastic top is suitable for a table on which spills may occur, such as a bed stand, dressing table, etc. A solid wood table top which can be polished is advantageous on a work table.

CHAIRS AND ARMCHAIRS

Is the chair comfortable?

Try it out—thoroughly. The normal seat height is $17^{1}/_{2}$", but it is better to take a chair which is too low rather than too high. Try the chair at a table. Choose the chair first, then the table. Do the back and arms afford real support?

How is the seat made?

The padding may rest on a support of plywood, webbing or springs, each resulting in a different degree of softness. Test each to determine which suits you best.

How strong is the chair?

The true durability can be ascertained only by subjecting the chair to a chair-testing machine. However, the chair's measurements can give you some clue. If the chair's frame is fragile, the tenons where the pieces join together will be small. This makes crosspiece braces between the chair legs absolutely necessary, especially between the front and back legs. The pegs and braces ought to be particularly sturdy at the point of juncture, so that the tenons can be sufficiently large. Check the chair underneath. The blocks at the corners should be strong.

Is the material good?

If there are any curved parts, notice whether they are sawed out of the wood or bent. Bent wood is stronger, because the wood fibers remain intact. If the curved piece is executed by sawing, then the fibers have been severed.

Is the chair nicely made?

Softly rounded edges, all accessible surfaces well finished and tight joints are all signs of good craftsmanship. From an esthetic point of view it is best if the grain of the wood follows the line of the furniture instead of going counter to it; furthermore the grain in the four legs of a table or chair should be similar.

SOFAS AND EASY CHAIRS

Is it comfortable? Chair backs have varying angles of inclination suitable for varying uses—work, relaxation, conversation, or coffee drinking. Try out the sitting height, the neck support, and arm rests for comfort.

Is it durable? Here again it is difficult to know without scientific tests, but one can see whether the arm rests and frame seem stable. Is it nicely made? The upholstery should be smooth with straight, secure corners. No creaking should be audible. The pattern of the fabric and the shape of the furniture should be coordinated, and all the seams should be even.

Design in general Remember, even a comfortably big easy chair ought to be easy to move.

BEDS

Is the bed big enough? Mattresses are normally $35^{1}/_{2}'' \times 77''$. The inside length of the bed should exceed the body length by 8".

Is the height correct? In a bedroom a bed should be $21^{1}/_{2}''$-$23^{1}/_{2}''$ high. Then it is easy to make. If the bed has long legs it is easy to clean under. A bed which is also used for sitting purposes should be no higher than 18", with legs at least 10" long.

Design The quality of the bed should come first, and then its appearance.

CUPBOARDS, BUREAUS AND BOOK SHELVES

What do you want to store? Try to estimate the quantity. How many shelves are needed? Are there any bulky items?

Are the measurements correct? Most "shelf-type articles" need $12'' \times 18''$ (bed sheets need $21^{1}/_{2}''$, but somewhat larger shelves are better). Good multi-purpose cupboard shelf sizes are $12'' \times 21^{1}/_{2}''$ and $17^{1}/_{2}'' \times 21^{1}/_{2}''$. For book shelves fiction needs at least 7" deep non-fiction $9^{1}/_{2}''$, and scrapbooks, and such, at least $10^{1}/_{2}''$.

Shallow or deep cupboard?	Area and wall space determine whether one should choose a shallow and wide or a deep and narrow cupboard. A deep cupboard should be equipped with shallow drawers.
Room for growth?	Can similar sections be added to the cupboard in various directions? It is always an advantage if a number of cupboards can be placed together. The furnishing is then more simple and orderly.
Is the material good?	The kind of wood used in the veneer is mainly a question of taste. The underlying wood must be of good quality, especially when it comes to book shelves, which must not bend, and cupboard doors, which must not warp.
Is it nicely made?	Check to be sure the drawers and doors function properly and that the locks work. Well finished details are often an indication of quality throughout.

The above shopping advice is based on information given by Erik Berglund and Sten Engdal, who direct the function studies for the Swedish Society for Industrial Design.

Scandinavian Homes and their Furnishings

Furnishing a home is applied democracy. The aim should be to achieve a functional, socially well motivated and esthetically attractive whole in which the interests of every member of the family are looked after as far as possible without destroying the mutual framework. One must be aware of one's own needs in order to pick out what is personally suitable from the enormous selection of products offered by an affluent society.

In Scandinavia, social studies of family and home have succeeded in outlining at least a preliminary picture of the family and its life together. This information has been used to advantage in the production of homes and furnishings. The picture is not uniform, and there is great variation in the make-up of homes. As in other corners of the world, there is a tendency in Scandinavia to be swayed by the vast amount of material in magazines concerning interior decoration; and subsequently the home is furnished to make an attractive "picture" rather than a functional interior. It is constructed more for the eyes than for the body. Knowledge concerning man's measurements, the function of the household, materials and construction is not always utilized in the way it should be.

The "two-house family" has a rather long tradition in Scandinavia, and the rising affluence makes it possible for an ever greater number of people to possess a summer or vacation place as well as their regular dwelling. In the following two sections we present interiors, and furniture intended for the permanent household—town house or city apartment—as well as for the vacation retreat. We have tried to make the choice as many-sided and varied as possible, in order to illustrate how freely and personally a home can be furnished if one makes use of all the possibilities offered by the rich Scandinavian furniture market.

The Scandinavian home tries to be practical and functional, but at the same time pleasant and adaptable to the interests of the whole family. The main thing is that it does its job. In order to facilitate as many of the home's activities as possible, the Swedish furniture designer Sune Fromell has designed a furniture series called "Växa" (Grow), for the Co-operative Society. It consists of a number of units which can be combined in a variety of ways and used for a variety of purposes. The large picture shows how desk space for young and old can be arranged in the home with the aid of this furniture. In the small picture, several of the units from the series have been utilized to make a sewing spot for the lady of the house.

Spindle-back chairs are the most common chairs in the Scandinavian furniture production. The lathed details can be kept to a minimum, and almost every self-respecting furniture designer has produced a variation of this chair. This is Carl Malmsten's "Åland". The interior is respesentative of practical-minded simplicity—not without subtlety—and a touch of Spartan contempt for comfort which can be found in the Scandinavian setting.

The color photo shows a collection of furniture designed by different Nordic architects. Left: a day bed by the Swede Bruno Mathsson. The table is designed by the Finn Alvar Aalto and the metal chairs by the Dane Verner Panton. The curtains are a composition of the Swedish artist Dagmar Lodén and the lamp is from Le Klint, Denmark.

Wood with a "living" surface, color-coordinated materials with a coarse texture, and visual contact with the wide expanse of the garden put their mark on this architect's home in Helsinki. The two armchairs covered with yellow fabric were designed by Carl-Johan Boman, Finland's grand old man in the art of furniture making. Scandinavian "togetherness" is indicated by the fact that the two light armchairs are the work of the Dane Ib Kofod-Larsen. The furniture fabrics were composed and produced by Marjatta Metsovaara. The teak table was designed by Eric Johann, for Askon Tehtaat. The wall tapestry composed by Elsa Montell-Saarnio. The grill forks and poker are by Bertel Gardberg, Finland's leading silversmith. Welded iron relief is by sculptor Eila Hiltunen.

Interior of a vacation retreat, created by Anne-Lise Aas, who also designed the individual pieces of furniture and the textiles. The atmosphere in this room is typical of the moderate modernism which is currently affecting the ideal for the Norwegian vacation retreat.

One of Europe's most up-to-the-minute luxury homes is the estate, outside Paris, of art dealer Louis Carré. It was designed by the Finn Alvar Aalto. His feeling for material and expressive forms can be distinguished down to the smallest details. With the help of custom-made furniture—exclusive variations of his well-known standard pieces—Aalto has produced an interior with great character. It should be observed that this millionaire's home differs only in degree and not in character from the most modest everyday interiors which are the work of this same architect.

The most advanced Danish private homes are usually extremely austere and sparse in their furnishings. To a large extent, the place gets its character from expressive architectonic materials. The rest of the furnishings are intended only to meet the elementary practical requirements. But, as the picture shows, the room has no dogmatic modernism. In the right foreground a bureau of an older type can be glimpsed. The Danish interior decorators have a remarkable ability to combine the old and new in an unconventional manner.

Safari chairs are by Kaare Klint, and in right background is a chair by Poul Kjærholm.

This double-page spread shows two dining room arrangements, both carried out by Swedish interior decorator Thea Leonhard. She likes to run the gamut of Scandinavian furniture in her interiors. Facing page: chairs by the Dane Arne Jacobsen, manufactured by Fritz Hansens Eft. A/S. Hanging over the table is the famous "tefat" (saucer) by Poul Henningsen, the Danish design pioneer. Below are chairs designed by Thea Leonhard and manufactured by Nesto, Sweden.

A selection of everyday wooden chairs. Left: bar stool by the Finn Alvar Aalto. The seat is not solid wood but made of plywood on a round frame. Above: spindle-back chair designed by the Swede Sonna Rosén, for Nesto. Opposite page, top left: chairs and stool by the Finn Olof Ottelin, for Stockmann. Next to these: chairs designed by the Finn Olavi Hänninen, for Huonekaluliike Mikko Nupponen. Below: chair of the "jærbu" type designed by the Norwegian Alf Sture and manufactured by Edv. Wilhelm Moelv.

77

Armchair with footstool and end table in oak, designed in 1960 by the Dane Börge Mogensen, for Fredericia Stolefabrik. The furniture fabric and rug were designed by Börge Mogensen and Lis Ahlmann, for A/S C. Olesen's Cotil collection. Over a period of more than ten years, Börge Mogensen has succeeded in persuading a number of Danish firms and one Swedish furniture firm to produce furniture of a very high quality of workmanship, thanks to exceptional pedagogic patience.

Chair (in teak or oak) by Hans J. Wegner, for C. M. Madsens Fabrikker, Denmark. Even to this simple, traditional chair Wegner has added his personal touch in the form of a boldly modelled top rail that melts beautifully into the chair arms.

Interior by Ilmari Tapiovaara, Finland. Furniture is made of fir with soapstone base and leather cushions, produced by Askon Tehtaat. Tapiovaara also designed the two lamps against the back wall for the same firm.

Some Danish architects specialize in practical utility with simple, well thought out construction, but the manner of execution is rather delicate and exclusive. Mahogany library chair with seat of webbing by Mogens Koch, for Rud. Rasmussens Snedkerier. Mogens Koch got his inspiration for this refined folding chair from a newspaper clipping showing General Patton's headquarters during the war. When the chair is folded up, all the parts lie between the two broad side pieces. When the seat is open, the broad stretcher or horizontal brace in the lower frame can be used as a ladder, if one wants a book which is on a shelf out of normal reach. In the background can be seen some of the shelves designed by Mogens Koch in 1928 for Rud. Rasmussens Snedkerier. The rug "Sandrevler" (sandbanks) is designed by Mogens Koch and hand made by his wife, Ea.

Many of the Scandinavian furniture designers have tried their hand at metal furniture. Above left: a sample of latest chair type by the Dane Poul Kjærholm. The leather cover can be pulled off the plastic frame very simply. The chair is produced by E. Kold Christensen. Next to this is a little leather-covered chair on a metal tube stand, designed by the Norwegian Tormod Alnæs, for Norway Designs A/S. Both chairs on the left are designed by the Swedish furniture pioneer Axel Larsson, for Verkstads AB Lindqvist. Larsson has played a prominent part during the last three decades in the development of Swedish standard furniture. The sculptural chair shown on facing page is designed by the Finn Antti Nurmesniemi, for Oy Merivaara Oy.

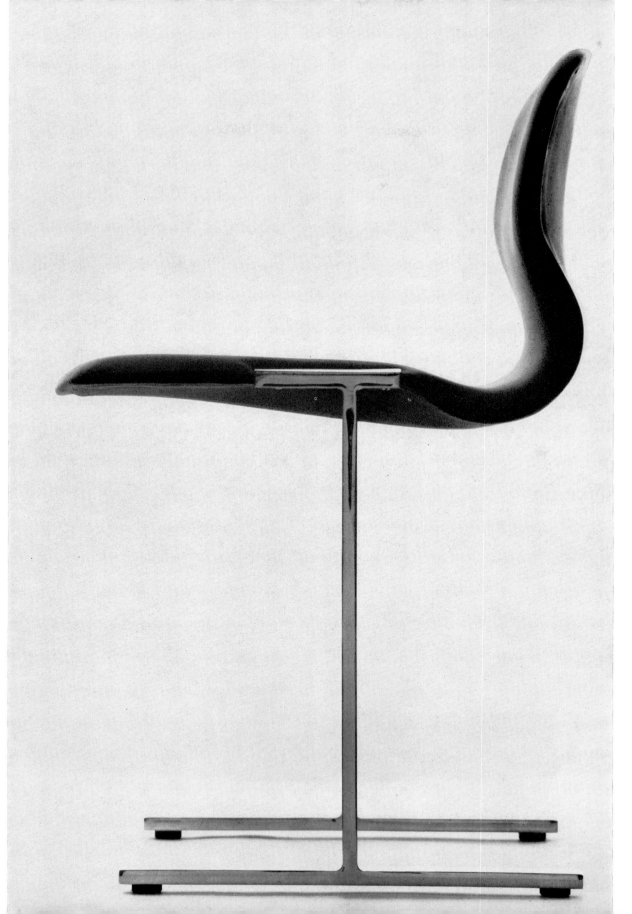

The chair on the left illustrates the inventiveness of Hans J. Wegner. Produced by Getama A/S, Denmark, it is made of about 230 meters of ordinary flag cord, which is stretched without breaks or knots over a steel tube frame. The two loose ends are tied in a knot under the chair. Wegner's intention is that one should put a pelt on the chair if one is bothered by drafts.

Two Danish architects, Ejner Larsen and A. Bender Madsen, have produced the chair on the right by working with master carpenter Willy Beck. Both architects have concentrated on a few types of chairs which they have consistently developed and improved over the years. The chair shown has a bow-shaped top rail of molded plywood which is covered with leather. The hourglass shape of the piece in the seat frame provides a large surface at the juncture with the chair legs. At the same time it gives the stretched leather a comfortable bowl shape.

The Dane Ole Wanscher has mastered many different types of furniture, which are a result of his thorough study of 18th-century English furniture. Wanscher's furniture is polished and aristocratic throughout. The elegant top rail on the chair consists of two pieces of wood glued together, giving it a stability that would be impossible if it had been carved from a single piece of wood.

The chair on this page is the design of Torbjörn Afdal and was produced by Bruksbo A. S., Norway. The detail photo above shows how carefully the design has been worked out.

Physiological studies have shown
that a chair need not be upholstered or voluminous in order
to be comfortable. Most Scandinavian chairs are a reasonable
size. At left is one of the most
comfortable, an armchair with
foot stool by the Swede Yngve
Ekström, for Swedese. The Dane
Hans J. Wegner was in an extra-
vagant mood when he designed
the munificent easy chair on the
facing page for A. P. Stolen as a
sitting device for an affluent society. Above: chair designed by
Bendt Winge, Norway, for Jacob
Låthe, and armchair by the Norwegian Fredrik A. Kayser, for
Vatne Lenestolfabrik.

Left: the large photo shows a typically airy and practical bedroom interior in a modern Scandinavian home. The Swede Bertil Fridhagen designed the furniture for AB Svenska Möbelfabrikerna. Below: bed in tubular steel designed by Hans Kempe and Lars Ljunglöf, Sweden.

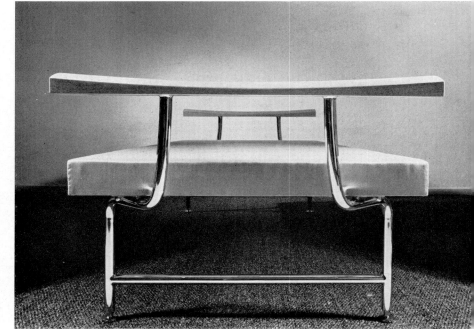

Viennese architect Josef Frank, who has worked in Sweden for the past 30 years, introduced the polish and grace of the Viennese style into Nordic furniture art. The picture on the opposite page shows a bedroom corner furnished by Frank. The furniture was manufactured by Svenskt Tenn.

A Danish interior stamped with Kaare Klint's classic modernism.

The Swedish Society of Rural Communes is blazing the trail for the production and distribution of furniture especially intended for use by older people with diminished strength and agility. Furniture pioneer Carl Malmsten and his son Vidar, at the request of the Society, have designed a complete series of furniture to be used in homes for the aged. Every detail of the furniture has been thought out in terms of the old people's requirements. This furniture also shows the characteristic form of the master. See also the next pages.

95

Both furniture groups by Carl and Vidar Malmsten on these pages are taken from Swedish homes for the aged. Notice the relatively high sofa seats, the straight, firm back rests and the arm rests that curve upward. All of these details are meant to facilitate use by older people. At the same time, the interiors have an unmistakable Scandinavian touch and bear witness to a consistent household culture.

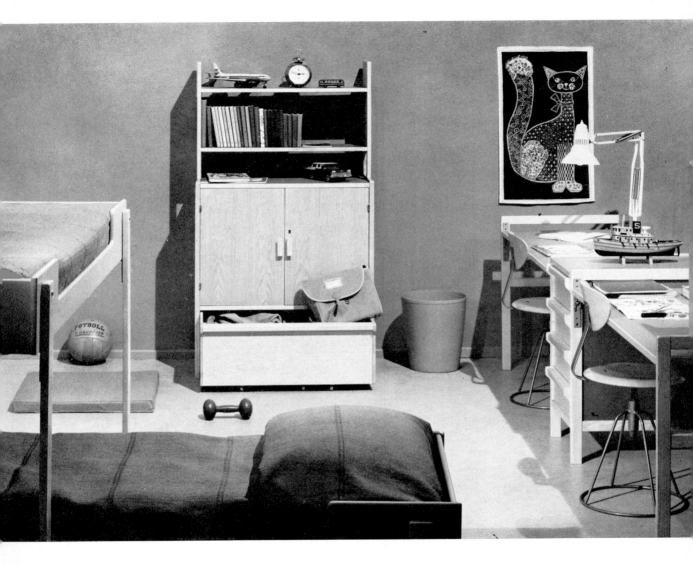

Furniture for children and young people has also come in for its share of attention in Scandinavia. Left: an interior utilizing Sune Fromell's furniture series "Växa med Läxa" (Grow while learning) for the Cooperative Society. The furniture can be expanded as the child grows. Bottom left: rocking chair by Erik Höglund for Boda. Kristian Vedel of Denmark designed the little plywood children's chair for Torben Örskov & Co. His countrymen, Nanna and Jörgen Ditzel, designed the high chair for A/S Kolds Savværk.

The Swede Stefan Gip's furniture for children, the BA-series for Skrivrit, is one of the most interesting. It is based on comprehensive studies of the body measurements of 2—6 year-olds, made at the child psychology department of the pedagogical institute of Stockholm University. The furniture bears a product declaration and has been durability tested. It should be mentioned that the children's chair has been teetered 87,000 times with the abnormal load of 154 lb., without the least sign of weakness.

The Vacation Retreat

When the winter sun glistens on the mountains, the Norwegian takes his skiis and heads for his cabin or for a mountain hotel, both of which are furnished in a characteristically robust way. In the summertime the Danes move out to their small, cosy cottages on the coast or in the softly rolling countryside. The Swedes flee to their cabins in the archipelago or to the forests and fishing waters. If one looks out over the sober, Finnish pine forest landscape with its thousands of lakes on a Saturday evening, one can see smoke rising from countless fires heating up the typical Finnish steambaths. There are probably few places in the world where people are so fascinated by nature, and where there is so much unspoiled nature. With some justification Scandinavia has been described as Europe's vacation spot of the future.

This is why a home for leisure time plays such an important role in Scandinavia and why so much attention is paid to its furnishing. Often this house is adapted to local tradition and consciously furnished in a rustic or primitive manner, in order to intensify the contrast between life there and life in the city or town. Of course, to an ever greater extent, efficient, series-produced cottages, with all the modern conveniences, are appearing; but even in these there are many features which can, with good reason, be called Scandinavian.

Finishing off the parade of pictures of Scandinavian homes and furnishings is a small selection of these vacation retreats and the furnishings which are often made expressly for them. Not infrequently one finds that these vacation retreats are more personally furnished than the more standardized city dwellings. This is partially explained by the fact that considerations of social prestige are not of the same consequence when it comes to a summer home. In recent years, a need to satisfy more basic functions has also entered into the question. During leisure time the simple, important things become tangible.

One often encounters an unconventional and carefully considered combination of old and new in the best interiors in Scandinavian vacation retreats. This Danish interior contains, among other things, two classic chairs by Kaare Klint and a leather easy chair, "Ægget" (The Egg), by Arne Jacobsen.

100

The photos on these pages show interiors from the summer homes
of two famous Swedish architects. The one is located on the coast
and the other in the archipelago. Both architects have made use of
older existing buildings. In furnishing, they have retained the old-
fashioned feeling but supplemented the existing furniture with new
pieces. Even a radically modern, industrially-produced chair, like
Arne Jacobsen's "Myran" (The Ant), blends into the traditional
setting. It should be emphasized that both architects are decidedly
progressive. At the same time, they feel it is important to preserve
the value inherent in old furnishing cultures as a contrast to the
standardized modern way of life.

Some architects go completely modern in their summer homes; nevertheless, they still succeed in maintaining contact with natural, robust functionalism. Below: interior done by the Dane Börge Mogensen. At right: sleeping quarters in the Swede Bruno Mathsson's extremely modern summer home.

Alf Sture of Norway furnished this harmonious summer dining room with furniture he designed himself. Produced by Hiort & Östlyngen, it harks back to the robust Norwegian tradition.

Out of the enormous collection of leisure-time furniture we have chosen these two specimens. Left: folding chair by the Swede Gunnar Eklöf, for Hantverket. Right: hanging basket chair by the Danes Nanna and Jörgen Ditzel, for R. Wengler.

The classic deckchair in Scandinavian furniture production was designed by the Dane Kaare Klint, in the early 30's, for Rud. Rasmussens Snedkerier. It appeared after extensive studies of different resting positions, and helped greatly to increase respect for function studies in furniture production. After 30 years the chair still retains its validity.

Norwegian architect Björn Ianke, as a pupil of Carl Malmsten, has carried on the genuine Scandinavian furniture tradition in Norway. The color photo shows an interior from the upper story of his summer home, "Fisherman's rest," on the Norwegian coast. On the lower floor Ianke has his carpentry workshop, and here he has made all of the furnishings for the upper floor, from stairs to furniture and picture frames.

The Modern Movement in Scandinavia

DENMARK

Exquisite handling of wood, scrupulous construction, and restrained design are considered characteristics of Danish handicraft furniture. In recent years, however, several of the leading designers have successfully created furniture of a decidedly industrial nature, making use of metal and plastic, among other things.

It is often said, and quite rightly so, that the Danish handicraft tradition has been an extremely significant factor in the extraordinarily rapid development of the new Danish furniture art. It should not be overlooked that, right from the start, the conditions essential for modern furniture production, theoretical precepts and social goals, were clearly formulated in accordance with the new times. In 1910 there was already an independent furniture art in Denmark, with choice designs, good construction, and excellent cabinetwork. But in the 1920's and 30's architect Kaare Klint laid down the fundamental principles for current developments. In 1924 he was made a professor at the newly established furniture school of the Danish Academy of Art. As early as 1916 Klint had executed sketches for storage furniture of a radical new type which presaged his later development. In his lectures he initiated an entirely new theoretical point of departure concerning furniture design. Empty, formalized sketches with preconceived ideas about the final result, were totally foreign to him. The starting point was always to determine what the job involved, a study of the human proportions in relation to the thing, space needed, construction possibilities, dimensions, and treatment of material. His original solutions were based on thorough, careful planning. He concentrated on the heart of the item, not its shell. His principles embraced and enlarged upon the classic traditions. On one occasion he said, "The ancients were more modern than we." To him "modern" was synonymous with a well-done, consistent job. Chinese, Egyptian, Gothic, baroque, rococo and Empire influences

Architect Werner West has played an important role as intermediary between the old and new milieu concepts in Finland. He designed the green chairs for Kerava Snickeri. The corner cupboard is characteristic of the so-called Åbo Renaissance. The "Rya" rug is from the 18th century, and the ultra-modern lamps are by Tapio Wirkkala and Lisa Johansson-Pape.

113

are found in Klint's work. However, what he sought was not characteristics of style but the fundamentals common to these different styles. If he felt that a certain old model could not be improved, then he saw no reason for changing it. On this subject he has said, "An aversion for old things leads to a loss of perspective and excludes the best help one can get: building on experience acquired over hundreds of years. There are no problems that have not been solved many times before."

Klint was also a pioneer when it came to using wood in a natural way. He was an avid student of nature—originally an artist—and in nature nothing is painted or varnished. Wood should always be itself. He preferred untreated wood, undyed leather, and textiles with white, grey, brown or black wool.

In 1927 a step was taken which was to have the greatest consequences on future developments. The Copenhagen Cabinetmakers Guild, which is more than 400 years old, decided to arrange an annual exhibition of good handicraft furniture. The immediate motivation was the unemployment crisis and the threat posed by emerging industrialization. Since 1930, a contest for new types of furniture has been organized in conjunction with this annual exhibit. During the first years, the cabinetmakers were sharply criticized for their old-fashioned designs. In response to this criticism they started working with a number of young furniture designers. The realization of the new furniture ideal can be traced to this close cooperation between the cabinetmakers and their designers. Because of this the cabinetmakers' eyes were opened to the designs of the day. And the designers, for their part, learned to work with manufacturers and learned to meet the technical demands of the craftsman. The best entries from the annual Cabinetmakers' contest were made up and shown at the exhibition the following year. This emphasized still further the cooperation between designer and craftsman. The significance of the exhibition lay in the fact that it acted as a catalyst for something positive. It served a purpose over and beyond the commercial, and in this way became a cultural implement. Year after year, new furniture with new constructions and new materials has been shown at these exhibitions. Copenhagen's Cabinetmakers Guild has become a training school for young architects and an influencial source of energy even for international furniture art.

At first industry followed the lead of handicraft, used the same designers, and produced simplified versions of handicraft furniture. This course of action was criticized, because the manufacturers were not considering sufficiently the true needs of the consumer. As a result of this, the furniture industry initiated studies of household habits. These proved the critics correct and gave rise to alterations in production. In recent years the industrial concerns have organized regular annual exhibitions patterned after those of the Cabinetmakers.

One reason for the immediate success of the new line of industrial furniture was an extensive information program pushing more modern interior decoration in the homes. Interest on the part of the public grew by leaps and bounds. One must also keep in mind that the world-famous handicraft furniture which has met with such a ready market in different foreign countries, especially the United States, is so expensive that it can be sold only to a very limited extent on the home market. Industrial production—more important from the point of view of the average consumer—is of a less exclusive sort and on the whole more realistic. It cannot be denied that in recent years the gap has widened between the exclusive, esthetic, handicraft furniture and the less expensive, realistic, everyday furniture.

Of special importance for the household standard in Denmark has been the fact that the Danish Cooperative Society (FDB) had already started producing inexpensive, practical furniture at the end of the 30's. FDB is Denmark's biggest retail organization, and its furniture is found in many homes, especially in the countryside, where it has paved the way for better home furnishings.

Besides Kaare Klint some of the furniture architects of the 30's who deserve special mention are: O. Mölgaard-Nielsen, Arne Jacobsen, Ole Wanscher, Rigmor Andersen and Edvard and Tove Kindt-Larsen. A new generation appeared at the end of the 30's and beginning of the 40's; and among these Hans J. Wegner, Börge Morgensen, Finn Juhl and Peter Hvidt can be named. Hvidt often works with Mölgaard-Nielsen.

But it is really two architects, Hans J. Wegner and Finn Juhl, who put their stamp on Danish furniture design at the end of the 40's and the beginning of the 50's. Wegner is himself a trained and skillful cabinetmaker. Often his models evolve from a quick sketch made in the studio, followed by a session in the workshop, where he personally produces the piece in detail. The original model often undergoes changes during the process, and, like a sculptor, Wegner does not leave his creation until he has achieved the form he wants.

Finn Juhl, on the other hand, has to some extent opposed the functional and anonymous furniture types of Kaare Klint. He is a subjectivist, and regards furniture as modern sculpture, in which the play of lines expresses values akin to those of abstract art. He often imbues his furniture with an elegant and soaring touch.

In recent years Börge Mogensen has attained a position of prominence. With the greatest consistency he pursues the Kaare Klint line. As mentioned on page 54, he has had great success with built-in cabinets, as well as other furniture based on important function studies. Börge Mogensen does not start with a preconceived artistic idea when designing for function and construction to take this line of action. He practices what he calls the "workshop method" —which means that, by tirelessly sorting and coordinating all the demands one might make on a piece of furniture, he will arrive at a lucid design. This is clear proof of the respect he has for the consumer.

Two architects, namely Arne Jacobsen and Poul Kjærholm, have worked successfully with materials other than wood. Jacobsen is one of Scandinavia's leading architects and a proponent of a polished, minutely worked out, light and elegant style of construction. These traits are also apparent in his furniture. Jacobsen has unfailingly made the most of the possibilities offered by industrial production. Kjærholm constructs his furniture on a metal frame. He is greatly interested in the relative expressive values of construction, and combines metal with materials such as leather and rattan. His style of furniture is distinguished by clarity and absolute consistency.

At this writing, a heated debate is in progress concerning the goals of Danish furniture production. One group contends that our new social structure and the rising standard of living of the consumer should result in greater freedom for the designer than is allowed by earlier social-ethical program drawn up in the spirit of Kaare Klint. This group is hoping for less asceticism and generally freer artistic forms. It is true, no doubt, that designers should be able to enlarge upon their furniture forms in the future. But at the same time, one must keep in mind that furniture is meant essentially to serve; it follows that our surroundings should be enriched primarily with the help of textiles, top-notch applied art and fine art.

FINLAND

Finland experienced an artistic heyday during the years before and just after the turn of the century. It found expression in, among other things, a production of the more exclusive type of furniture. A number of the leading architects of the period, Eliel Saarinen and Lars Sonck, for example, designed furniture that bore the unmistakable mark of their forceful styles. These attempts were fairly isolated phenomena, however, since the main intent of the architects was to create furniture which expressed their own personal views on the national traits. In the Iris factory, Finland's first producer of industrial art, Louis Sparre created from 1897 to 1902 excellent furniture of a type similar to the art nouveau style in England and Austria at that time. Of greater importance on the purely practical level was the work of furniture designers Carl Johan Boman and Werner West in the 1910's and 20's. They acted as the intermediaries between an older generation and the new stream of functionalism. Boman, who is still active, is the grand old man of Finland's furniture art.

Carl Johan Boman possesses an exceptional fund of knowledge about the production of furniture, from the handicraft as well as the technical side. On the technical end he has been a pioneer of some consequence. Boman has designed chairs, for example, which can be adjusted to different sitting positions by means of a simple device. He has constructed stackable chairs, folding chairs, and row chairs. And he has focused much of his attention on space-saving furniture for the small modern apartment. Boman has also often worked on the interior decoration of ships, and from this experience in a special field that is so rigidly bound by function he has gleaned important knowledge applicable to his other production.

The real breakthrough for a radically modern furniture style came with Alvar Aalto. First and foremost a building architect with impressive accomplishments, Aalto has also designed a number of truly original pieces of furniture. Aalto's bent wood birch table and chairs from the early 30's possess the simple and effective form associated with the first functionalism. They are simultaneously robust and elegant, and have remained on the market practically unaltered since then. They are often held up as an excellent example of modern furniture that rises above the fashion dictates of the day in the hectic hunt for novelties. Aalto appeared on the scene just as Finland's new wood industry was springing up. The new plywood fulfilled one condition for the production of chair types designed expressly for industrial manufacture.

Aalto's furniture has interesting details which can be singled out. Especially worthy of notice is his method of shaping the juncture of the vertical and horizontal elements where chair or table legs connect with the seat or table top. Aalto has called the furniture leg the baby sister of the architectonic column. He lets the leg join the table top in a soft arch like a hand with fingers. This gives an organic, coalescent character to the vertical and horizontal elements of the furniture. Stools and small chairs are perhaps the best and most distinctive things in Aalto's production. He has also design-ed a series of children's furniture, with kindergartens and day nurseries especially in mind. They can be combined and stacked, and have been widely distributed in Finland.

Two main lines of development are clearly distinguishable in Finland's current furniture production. One pursues the vigorous tradition of wood, chiefly birch. The other makes use of steel con-struction, often of a very advanced type. The first group employs material of a relatively coarse dimension in order to underscore the stable and reassuring character of the furniture, even though, from a purely technical point of view, this is not always called for. Birch is a solid and supple wood which lends itself to very lithe dimensions.

Olavi Hänninen is an excellent designer of wood furniture. He was a teacher in the furniture department of Atheneum, the in-dustrial arts school. Over the years he has arrived at an extremely simplified furniture style which is stable and rugged. Among the designers of the young generation, Reino Ruokolainen achieved a prominent position during recent years with his H-line. The asceti-cism of the H-line construction is original, but at the same time it has certain basic tendencies in common with the newer trends in Scandinavian design. A very pronounced horizontal effect is what Ruokolainen is trying to achieve in his furniture. The versatile furniture architect Olof Ottelin has made some very valuable contributions as a designer for the well-known Stockmann depart-ment store. Ottelin's furniture fits in very nicely with the general Scandinavian-type product. It is practical, unpretentious and refin-ed. Carl Gustav Hiort af Ornäs occupies a special position. He was originally a technician and worked mostly on solutions to struc-tural problems of design. Among other things, he has developed a method of bending plywood. Hiort af Ornäs has started his own production of quality furniture and acts as his own designer. Runar Engblom's carefully worked out and finely proportioned handicraft wood furniture has also made its contribution.

The pioneer in the metal group is Ilmari Tapiovaara. He is a versatile designer, greatly absorbed by the problems affecting industrial production. He has studied the stackability of chairs, their disassembly possibilities, and other related question. He works with a bent wood technique reminiscent of Alvar Aalto, but has specialized in metal and plastic furniture. During recent years Tapiovaara has designed furnishings for offices, hospitals, and other public buildings. Some of his work is done for the firm J. Merivaara Oy. Interior decorator Antti Nurmesniemi has designed notable chairs. He is otherwise known as one of Finland's best all-around designers. Olli Borg has made furniture in metal and plastic and can claim credit for the exquisite furnishings in the Palace Hotel in Helsinki. A young representative for the metal furniture line is Yrjö Kukkapuro. He is employed by the Moderno company and prefers to work with light, pliant furniture which can be used to advantage in waiting rooms, terraces, and so forth. The steel chairs often have plywood seats and backs, occasionally plastic. Moreover, it can be mentioned that ASKO, Scandinavia's largest furniture factory, uses Ilmari Tapiovaara and Tapio Wirkkala as their chief—free-lancers. The company's staff designers are Eric Johann, Jussi Peippo and Aulis Leinonen. ASKO's furniture pursues a popular line, is inexpensive but well-made, and designed in a simple and judicious manner. By producing good standard furniture, the two cooperative firms, OTK and SOK, have also done their bit, during recent years, toward furthering the sound, inexpensive, everyday article.

NORWAY

The older Norwegian furniture is characteristically heavy and robust. At the beginning of this century, a typical and romantic variation of the Jugend style appeared, the so-called dragonesque style. The foremost exponent of this style was Gerhard Munthe, Norway's first designer in the field of modern applied arts. The Norwegian furniture art went through a period of classicism in the 20's too, which was followed by functionalism in the 30's. Among the leading functionalistic furniture designers were Herman Munthe-Kaas and Knut Knutsen.

By oversimplifying things just a bit, one could say that the present-day furniture art in Norway is developing in three directions. On the one hand you find the robust national tradition, best expressed by the rustic furnishings of the "hytte"—the cabin in the mountains or by the sea—which plays such a big part in the Norwegian way of life. This practical, sturdy type of cabin furniture is a genre in itself. The more refined products, on the other hand, show certain influences from neo-classicism. The modern version has a stiff dignity well suited to the Norwegian tradition of the white-collar worker. The third trend is toward export furniture with a more international character.

The State School of Handicrafts and Industrial Art has helped tremendously to revive the Norwegian furniture art. Ever since the 40's, the leading furniture designers have come from this school. The designer who has managed to give the most individual modern interpretation of the old Norwegian tradition is Alf Sture. In the early 40's he helped to pave the way for a modern outlook and was one of the pioneers of the new furniture style in Norway. Recently, Sture has modified his position to some extent. Nowadays he likes to accentuate the traditional, and he reverts both to the more rustic style of furniture and the Norwegian white-collar tradition. Sture's theoretical point of view has been thoroughly thought out. His goal is to individualize his furniture and adapt it to the cosy comfort that we so sorely need in this rationalistic period. Much of his furniture is unaffected and warm. Sture thinks in wood, and he sculptures or gives his furniture dimensions that convey an impression of definite form. He strongly opposes superficial internationalism and shallow fashion. He has been honored with a number of official assignments.

Bendt Winge has a sound educational background both as carpenter and architect. He is one of the most versatile and conscientious designers, and his services as an intermediary conveying Scandinavian impulses to his countrymen have been of the utmost importance. Winge acted as consultant for the National Association of Norwegian Applied Arts for more than a decade, and in this way he exercised a great deal of pedagogical influence. He is, moreover, an interior decorating specialist, and has completed many jobs in an exemplary fashion. Winge is a sober, reasonable designer; he never lets quality and construction preclude elegance and ease. For many years, Torbjörn Afdal has been the head drafts-man for the Bruksbo company, and he has designed furniture which has been produced by more than 20 different factories. He is an unpretentious, matter-of-fact designer with a feeling for logic in the construction of wood furniture. Wood is his medium. Stylistically his work shows influences from such Danes as Kaare Klint and Ole Wanscher. Architects Rastad and Relling have the largest furniture firms in Oslo, and have designed much worthy furniture. In recent years they have turned their efforts toward a series of furniture, constructed according to a module system, which is suited to mass production and makes possible many combinations. Rastad and Relling have also worked on shelves, cupboards, and such. Now and then, in international shows, one runs across metal furniture designed by Tormod Alnæs. He is one of the foremost furniture architects of the in-between generation and a teacher at the State School of Handicrafts and Industrial Arts in Oslo.

Björn Ianke is one of the finest designers in Scandinavia, and he represents the most genuine Nordic traditions with his thor-oughly worked out and perfected furniture. Ianke is a former student of Carl Malmsten, but his production is entirely his own. Like Wanscher, he is a skilled cabinetmaker. The best of Ianke's work has originated in his own workshop, where he works with a model until it is full blown and consummate. He has carried out a number of interior decoration assignments with exclusive furni-ture and can be designated a specialist at giving an airy grace to comfortable "heavy" armchairs.

Sven Dysthe, one of the group of younger Norwegians, has had considerable success in recent years with his export furniture combining wood and metal. The furniture can be disassembled and is simple and comfortable, with a certain international look. Like many of his colleagues, Dysthe designs furniture for a num-ber of Norwegian manufacturers. Arne Halvorsen made a name for himself with superb arrangements at the furniture fair in Stavanger in 1961. He carried out the job with absolute purity and consistency. At the same fair, some of his individual pieces of furniture also attracted attention. The Stavanger fair was an important point in the career of Fredrik A. Kayser, too, although his furniture had won recognition earlier. Kayser is clearly mod-ern, employing simplified design and pure material effects.

On the whole, it seems as though the younger generation of

Norwegian furniture designers is bent on putting their country on a par with the rest of Scandinavia. This was brought out quite clearly at the above-mentioned furniture fairs in Stavanger, which were very successful.

SWEDEN

Current furniture production is more comprehensive and more differentiated in Sweden than in the other Scandinavian countries. It ranges all the way from the exclusive, handmade piece of wooden furniture to the industrially produced item in various materials. Truly modern furniture production developed first in Sweden, especially if one views it in connection with attempts to raise the household standards of the masses.

Two pioneers, both born in the 1880's and still active, are the guiding lights for this furniture art. Carl Malmsten gained recognition as early as 1916, when he won the competition for the interior decoration of the Stockholm Town Hall. Ever since then he has followed his own line with great consistency. Malmsten is simultaneously carpenter, designer, cultural historian, pedagogue, and passionate propagandist for what he calls "the Swedish inheritance." During the years when functionalism was fighting for recognition, he was regarded as an arch reactionary, because he violently attacked what he considered to be a sterile formalism. Today we can see that Carl Malmsten's criticism was correct in many respects. Uniform, one-track internationalism has long since passed its prime. Nowadays we strive to enrich the general international picture with our special national features. Undoubtedly, Malmsten has learned a lot from functionalism; but at the same time, he has achieved a fine balance between traditional and modern. He can be regarded as a fine intermediary between the old and new. He himself says that he has followed "the classic Swedish line of unpretentious simplicity for the furtherance of peace-filled home and work milieu."

Josef Frank, on the other hand, is completely international. He came originally from Vienna and belonged to the radical circle of architects found there during the 20's. Frank has been Scandinavia's most important exponent of the polished, gracious, and quality-conscious Viennese style. Although it is often overlooked, this style has had considerable influence on Scandinavian furniture forms. Josef Frank has shown that furniture art, in the true sense of the word, cannot be achieved by formulas. In the long run, the designer must have creative ability if he is going to produce pieces of furniture with character.

This did not prevent the Stockholm Exhibition of 1930—functionalism's big policy declaration in Scandinavia—from having a decided significance. The leading architects abandoned geometric functionalism and turned their attention to the creation of practical, utilitarian furniture. Architects like G. A. Berg, Einar Dahl and Axel Larsson tried to decrease the volume and weight of furniture and clear the "subscape" by fastening shelves and cupboards onto walls. These designers made progress in creating comfortable chairs by studying the sitting positions and neck supports and constructing the angle of the arm rests according to the arms and hands of the sitting person. They also systematically studied the possibilities of varying materials and colors in standard furniture with a view toward increasing the combination potentials. Bruno Mathsson is usually considered the most typical representative of this generation. He started to experiment with bent wood furniture about the same time as Alvar Aalto in Finland, and he quickly achieved the slender, elegant style which is now internationally renowned. Mathsson is not as extreme as Aalto in the matter handling wood. Among other things, this means he does not bend it as sharply as his colleague in Finland.

During the 40's, the basic ideas of functionalism were carried on by architects like Carl-Axel Acking and Elias Svedberg. Acking's activities range from exclusive handicraft to standard furniture. Svedberg's big contribution was the creation of the "Triva" series for Nordiska Kompaniet. To a large extent, these architects and their colleagues have based their designs on the results of the household and furniture function studies mentioned earlier. Gunnar Eklöf is another good example of this. Together with Dr. Bengt Åkerblom, he constructs chairs which are physiologically correct. Among the younger generations, Sune Fromell, for example, has constructed special furniture for children which can be raised or added to as they grow.

The special problems of industrial production have been studied by Alf Svensson at Dux, the foremost factory for upholstered furniture in Sweden. Karl Erik Ekselius works as both production chief and designer at J. O. Carlsson. He has managed to give a rare unity and distinction to the production there. Swedese offers an interesting example of coordinated production among a number of small factories. Yngve Ekström has been the source of design inspiration here.

The best example of coordinated resources over the whole field of interior decoration is afforded by the Bra Bohag (Good Household) group. Not only the furniture manufacturers, but even the producers of decorating textiles, carpets, and lamps, have pooled their resources in order to supplement and support each other on the market. Their mutual exhibitions have been carried out conscientiously and have had pedagogic value, helping to inform the public about good interior decoration.

Among the younger and youngest generations, there are a number of names that are already well established. Nils Strinning is known for his String series, in which he combined plastic-covered wire supports with wooden shelves. Sven Kai-Larsen is a specialist in institutional interior decoration with a vigorous and personal style. He has also executed extensive experiments with wooden office furniture composed of easily combinable standard elements. Hans Kempe and Lars Ljunglöf work independently on similar projects. An extraordinary designer with a fine feeling for wood and its potentials is John Kandell, a classicist in the young furniture art. Björn Hultén designs interiors with an artistic touch, and Hans Johansson has carried out some interesting experiments with wood construction without screws or glue; the tension of the material itself holds the various parts of the furniture together.

A number of the young architects just mentioned are members of a newly organized work-group consisting of eight furniture designers and eight prominent cabinetmakers. By close cooperation between the artists and artisans, this group hopes to create high-quality furniture of an experimental type, which can later be adapted to industrial production if it seems feasible. This enterprise is one of the most interesting aspects of Sweden's new furniture production, and can be regarded as a distinctive feature of the affluent society. Even though the need for sound everyday products has not been completely satisfied, there seems to be room for quality furniture of a more exclusive sort. One can quite easily imagine that the quality-conscious consumer will once again go to the skillful carpenter and order a chair. We exchange our car and washing machine when a better model appears on the market; but we choose top-quality furniture for our home to last a lifetime. Here, if ever, Gregor Paulsson's words are applicable: "Your choice means choosing a way of life."

Designers and Producers

This list comprises a selection of the most well known furniture designers and producers in Scandinavia.

Designers

DENMARK

Nanna Ditzel
Bydd. Hovedgade 332
Copenhagen

Peter Hjorth
Mariehöjvej 22
Copenhagen

Peter Hvidt
Valkendorfsgade 3
Copenhagen

Arne Jacobsen
Strandvej 413
Copenhagen

Finn Juhl
Sölvgade 38
Copenhagen

Arne Karlsen
Möllevæng 25—27
Copenhagen

Edvard & Tove Kindt-Larsen
Hvidörevej 14
Copenhagen

Poul Kjærholm
Rödovre Parkvej 290
Copenhagen

Mogens Koch
Kongens Nytorv 3
Copenhagen

Ejner Larsen
Muldvad 13
Copenhagen

Axel Bender Madsen
Muldvad 19
Copenhagen

Grethe Meyer
Jac. Lindbergsvej 17
Copenhagen

Börge Mogensen
Solösevej 37
Copenhagen

O. Mölgaard-Nielsen
Valkendorfsgade 3
Copenhagen

Ole Wanscher
Gotfr. Rodesvej 5
Copenhagen

Hans J. Wegner
Söndersövejen 30
Copenhagen

FINLAND

Alvar Aalto
Tegelb. 20
Helsinki

Carl-Johan Boman
Westend allén 77
Helsinki

Olli Borg
Topeliuksenkatu 7 a
Helsinki

Carl-Gustav Hiort af Ornäs
Tapiola Päivättärenp. 5
Päivätärst. Hagalund
Helsinki

Olavi Hänninen
Finnå
Hannika

Eric Johann
Vapaaniemi
Helsinki

Yrjö Kukkapuro
Kalevankatu 50 a
Helsinki

Aulis Leinonen
Runebergsgatan 41 a
Helsinki

Antti Nurmesniemi
Näätäkuja 4
Helsinki

Olof Ottelin
Karl Lindahlsvägen 3
Helsinki

Jussi Peippo
Hämeenkatu 16 A 17
Lahti

Reino Ruokolainen
Siilitie 1 Y 224
Helsinki

Ilmari Tapiovaara
Tallbergin Puistotie 6 B
Helsinki

Tapio Wirkkala
Morsviksvägen 3
Helsinki

NORWAY

Torbjörn Afdal
Uranienborgveien 6
Oslo

Tormod Alnæs
Ullevålsveien 5
Oslo

Sven Dysthe
Öygardveien 113 H
Bekkestua

Arne Halvorsen
Hegdehaugsveien 34
Oslo

Björn Ianke
Kongens Gate 2
Fredrikstad

Fredrik A. Kayser
Nadderudveien 103
Bekkestua

Rolf Rastad
Klingenberggaten 4
Oslo

Adolf Relling
Klingenberggaten 4
Oslo

Aage Schou
Bygdöy Allé 73
Oslo

Alf Sture
Incognitogaten 15 B
Oslo

Bendt Winge
Oscars gate 42
Oslo

SWEDEN

Carl-Axel Acking
Brahegatan 9
Stockholm

Einar Dahl
Valhallavägen 73
Stockholm

Gunnar Eklöf
Danderydsgatan 16
Stockholm

Karl Erik Ekselius
Långgatan 12
Vetlanda

Yngve Ekström
Vaggeryd

Josef Frank
Rindögatan 52
Stockholm

Sune Fromell
Farkostvägen 4
Lidingö

Björn Hultén
Götabergsgatan 20
Göteborg

Kerstin Hörlin-Holmquist
Kammakargatan 35
Stockholm

Hans Johansson
Gränsvägen 27 D
Västerhaninge

Sven Kai-Larsen
Riddargatan 42
Stockholm

John Kandell
Regeringsgatan 5
Stockholm

Hans Kempe
Österlånggatan 37
Stockholm

Axel Larsson
Runebergsgatan 5
Stockholm

Thea Leonhard
Köpmangatan 14
Stockholm

Lars Ljunglöf
Österlånggatan 37
Stockholm

Carl Malmsten
Strandvägen 5 B
Stockholm

Bruno Mathsson
Tånnögatan 17
Värnamo

Alf Svensson
Baltzarsgatan 30
Malmö

Erik Ullrich
Drottninggatan 59
Stockholm

Producers

DENMARK

Willy Beck
Classensgade 25
Copenhagen

Boligens Byggeskabe
ved C. Danel
Gl. Kongevej 124
Copenhagen

Bovirke
Falkonéralle 46
Copenhagen

E. Kold Christensen
Ole Nielsensvej 33
Copenhagen

France & Sön
Frederiksgade 13
Hilleröd

Fredericia Stolefabrik A/S
Prinsessegade 20
Fredericia

Fritz Hansens Eft. A/S
Dronningensgade 3
Copenhagen

Johannes Hansen
Bredgade 65
Copenhagen

Interna
Vodroffsvej 2 A
Copenhagen

A. J. Iversen
St. Kongensgade 124—126
Copenhagen

P. Jeppesen
Store Heddinge
Kolds Savværk
Kerteminde

P. Lauritsen & Sön
Ålestrup

C. M. Madsen
Hårby

Rud. Rasmussens Snedkerier
Nörrebrogade 45
Copenhagen

A. P. Stolen
Værkstedsvej 35
Copenhagen Valby

R. Wengler
Amager Torv 7
Copenhagen

Niels Vodder
Bille Brahesvej 2
Copenhagen

FINLAND

Artek
Keskuskatu 3
Helsinki

Askon Tehtaat Oy
Lahti

Haimi Oy Furniture Factory
Mannerheimintie 5
Helsinki

Heteka Oy
Nilsiänkatu 16—20
Helsinki

Pentti Jämsä & Co
Hämeenkatu 23
Lahti

Lahden Lapokalusto
Lahti

Lahden Puutyö Oy
Furniture Factory
Kirkkokatu 8
Lahti

J Merivaara Oy
Vanha Talvitie 11
Helsinki

Moderno
Kluuvikatu 3
Helsinki

Polsa Oy
Variokylä

Oy Wilh. Schauman AB
Jyväskylä

Sok Vaajakoski Factories
Vaajakoski

Sopenkorpi Oy
Furniture Manufacturers
Lahti

Tehokaluste Oy
Hallituskatu 15
Helsinki

NORWAY

Gustav Bahus Eftf. A/S
Os pr Bergen

Dokka Möbler
Dokka

Elverum Möbel- & Trevarefabrikk
Elverum

Hiorth & Östlyngen
Harbitz allé 5
Sköyen

A. Huseby & Co A/S
Möllergaten 6
Oslo

L. Jacobsens Möbelsnekkeri
Böchmannsgaten 11
Egersund

Möbelindustri A/S
Gjövik

Möbelindustri I/S
Egersund

Rasmus Solberg Möbelverksted
Ski

Karl Sörli & Sönner
Sarpsborg

Vatne Lenestolfabrikk
Vatne

SWEDEN

Abrahamssons Möbelfabrik AB
Smålands Taberg

AB Karl Andersson & Söner Möbelfabrik
Huskvarna

Bjästa Snickerifabriks AB
Bjästa

Bofyra AB
Ulricehamn

AB J. O. Carlsson
Vetlanda

AB Edsbyverken
Edsbyn

AB Eilas
Linköping

Gemla Fabrikers AB
Diö

Källemo Möbelfabrik AB
Vaggeryd

Ljungs Industrier AB
Malmö

Carl Malmsten AB
Strandvägen 5 B
Stockholm

Firma Karl Mathsson
Värnamo

Möbel-Konsum
Ringvägen 98
Stockholm

NK-Inredning
Hamngatan 5
Stockholm

AB Nässjö Stolfabrik
NESTO
Nässjö

Olof Perssons Fåtöljindustri
Jönköping

AB Seffle Möbelfabrik
Säffle

AB Skaraborgs Möbelindustri
Tibro

Stolfabriks AB
Smålandsstenar

String Design AB
Sorterargatan 11
Vällingby

Swedese Möbler AB
Vaggeryd

AB Svenska Möbelfabrikerna
Bodafors

Svenskt Tenn
Strandvägen 5 B
Stockholm

AB Hugo Troeds Industrier
Bjärnum

Ulferts Fabriker AB
Tibro

AB Westbergs Möbler
Tranås

Åfors Möbelfabriks AB
Blomstermåla

AB Åtvidabergs Industrier
Kungsträdgårdsgatan 20
Stockholm

Index

Photographers